SpringerBriefs in Population Studies

More information about this series at http://www.springer.com/series/10047

William P. O'Hare

The Undercount of Young Children in the U.S. Decennial Census

 Springer

William P. O'Hare
O'Hare Data and Demographic
   Services LLC
Ellicott City, MD
USA

ISSN 2211-3215   ISSN 2211-3223   (electronic)
SpringerBriefs in Population Studies
ISBN 978-3-319-18916-1   ISBN 978-3-319-18917-8   (eBook)
DOI 10.1007/978-3-319-18917-8

Library of Congress Control Number: 2015940976

Springer Cham Heidelberg New York Dordrecht London

Printed on acid-free paper

Springer International Publishing AG Switzerland is part of Springer Science+Business Media
(www.springer.com)

Acknowledgments

Much of the work reflected in this book was done while I was an American Statistical Association/National Science Foundation/U.S. Census Bureau research fellow working at the Census Bureau from the fall of 2011 to the fall of 2013. I want to thank these organizations for supporting me during this period. I would also like to thank the many colleagues at the Census Bureau who contributed to this work, including J. Gregory Robinson, Kirsten West, Jennifer Ortman, Eric Jensen, Melissa Scopilliti, Howard Hogan, Jason Devine, Deborah Griffin, Tommy Wright, Barbara Clark O'Hare and others too numerous to list. None of the organizations or individuals mentioned above are responsible for any errors or shortcomings in this manuscript.

Contents

Chapter 1
Introduction

Abstract The issue of census undercounts in the U.S. Census is introduced and background information on the issue of census accuracy is provided. An overview of the contents of the book is provided along with a description of the intended audiences. Uses of census data are discussed to provide readers with a sense of the importance of Census undercounts.

Keywords Census · Undercounts · Children · Census use

A passage from a 1940 U.S. Census report (Census Bureau 1944, p. 32), reads, "Underenumeration of children under 5 year old, particularly of infants under one year old, has been uniformly observed in the United States Census and in the Censuses of England and Wales and of various countries of continental Europe." With respect to the situation in the United States, this observation from more than 70 years ago is still largely true today. A recent report from an ad hoc U.S. Census Bureau Task Force on the Undercount of Young Children (Griffin 2014, p. I) concluded, "The undercount of children under age five in the Decennial Census, and in surveys like the American Community Survey (ACS), is real and growing." In the 2010 U.S. Census there was a net undercount of nearly a million children age 0–4 according to the Census Bureau's Demographic Analysis (O'Hare 2014c). Young children had the highest net undercount rate (4.6 %) of any age group by far.

Many people are surprised to learn that young children have a higher net undercount rate than any other age group. In the words of former Census Bureau Director Robert Groves (2010),

> It's often a surprise to many people when they learn that children tend to be undercounted in the US Censuses. Most can imagine various types of adults who fail to participate in Censuses, but don't immediately think of children being missed.

Daponte and Wolfson (2003, p. 2) also acknowledge the lack of recognition of Census undercounts of young children and state, "What is not well-recognized is that children tend to be undercounted at a rate greater than that of the general population."

W.P. O'Hare, *The Undercount of Young Children in the U.S. Decennial Census*,
SpringerBriefs in Population Studies, DOI 10.1007/978-3-319-18917-8_1

The undercount of young children is also inconsistent with much of the survey methodology literature which shows households with children are generally more likely to respond to a survey than households without children (Groves and Couper 1998; Brick and Williams 2012). Groves and Couper (1998, p. 138) offer this succinct summary of the relationship between children in the household and cooperation in survey research, "Without exception, every study that has examined response or cooperation finds positive effects of the presence of children in the household." However, it should be noted that there is no distinction made in Groves and Couper's review of the literature about the age of the children in the household. It should also be noted that a household response does not mean every person in the household is included in the response. A household could respond to the Census, for example, but fail to include a young child on the returned Census questionnaire.

It is also worth noting that the pattern of undercounts for young children in the Decennial Censuses, which is the focus of this book, is also seen in several major Census Bureau surveys. The Census Bureau's American Community Survey, Current Population Survey and Survey of Income and Program Participation all show lower coverage rates for young children compared to older children and adults (O'Hare and Jensen 2014; O'Hare et al. 2013). This suggests that the processes and mechanisms that lead to high net undercount rates for young children in the Census may also be operating in major surveys. This idea is not new or surprising. Martin (2007, p. 436) notes, "The same groups that are affected by coverage errors in the Census are also affected in demographic surveys conducted by the Census Bureau and other organizations." The fact that young children are under-reported in major Census Bureau surveys raises questions of whether there may be under-reporting of young children in other government surveys as well.

Despite the evidence regarding a long-standing net undercount of young children in the Census there has been little systematic examination of this issue by demographers, statisticians, or Census experts. There are no books on the undercount of children in the Census and my review of several books about the U.S. Census (Choldin 1994; Darga 1999; Skerry 2000; Anderson and Fienberg 2001; Prewitt 2003; and Hillygus et al. 2006) found only a few fleeting passages on the undercount of children in the Census. Not only is there very little information on this topic, much of what has been produced is in what is often called "fugitive research." For example, much of the data on the topic are in Census Bureau files or internal Working Papers at the Census Bureau or other organizations (West and Robinson 1999; Griffin 2014; Pitkin and Park 2005; O'Hare 1999, 2009, 2014a, b). In the sources that are most easily available, such as books and articles in scholarly journals, the topic is rarely covered or even acknowledged.

When Census coverage data have been made available in the past, information on children is usually a small part of a larger volume related to assessing the overall quality of Census counts (U.S. Census Bureau 1974; Fay et al. 1988; Robinson et al. 1993; Robinson and Adlakha 2002; Velkoff 2011; U.S. Census Bureau 2012). Because this information is difficult to find, the net undercount of young children is sometimes called the "overlooked undercount" (O'Hare 1999).

Ironically, those responsible for conducting the U.S. Census have often been unaware of the high net undercount of young children. A recent report by the U.S.

Census Bureau Task Force on the Undercount of Young Children (Griffin 2014, p. i) concluded, "The task force found that many of the managers working on the development of methods and the design of experiments and evaluation in 2010 were largely unaware of this undercount problem and especially the degree to which the problem existed in 2000." For example, in discussing the qualitative evaluations from the 2010 Census, a Census Bureau staff member (Griffin 2014, p. 16) stated, "...no one had highlighted this issue of undercounted young children as something worth studying so researchers did not optimize previous work to answer these questions."

Let me say a few words about nomenclature used in this publication. I use the term "children" to refer to the population age 0–17 and the term "young children" to refer to the population age 0–4. The term Census coverage is used to reflect both net undercounts and net overcounts. Unless otherwise noted, the term Census Bureau refers to the U.S. Census Bureau and the term Census refers to the U.S. Decennial Census. In some cases (often in the titles of tables or figures) I refer to differences rather than net undercounts or net overcounts because I think it more accurately communicates what is in the tables or charts. Also, in some places information is knowingly repeated so each Chapter is relatively free-standing.

1.1 Outline of the Book

The analysis presented here rests largely on the results of the Census Bureau's Demographic Analysis (DA) method for assessing Census accuracy. The DA method for measuring Census coverage is based on developing an independent estimate of the expected population, based largely on births and deaths, which is then compared to the Census counts. Demographic Analysis has a long of history of being used to assess the quality of the U.S. Census (Robinson 2010). I am convinced that DA is the best method available for estimating the net undercount of young children for two reasons. First, it relies on the cohort-component method which is one of the most widely used estimation techniques in demography. Secondly, the underlying data (largely vital events records) are widely viewed as very accurate. The reasons for focusing on the results of Demographic Analysis rather than other methods are explained in more detail in Chap. 2. A detailed explanation of the DA methodology is also provided in Chap. 2.

In Chap. 3, DA estimates for children are compared to the 2010 Census counts to detect net undercounts and overcounts. Results are examined by single-year of age, sex, race and Hispanic Origin for the population age 0–17. That leads to a focus on the population age 0–4 where the net undercount rate is the highest. The net Census coverage of young children is contrasted to that of adults and older children.

Chapter 4 provides historical data on the coverage of children in the U.S. Census from 1950 to 2010. The focus here is on the net undercount of young children compared to adults and older children. The differences between the undercount experiences of young children compared to older children are often larger than the difference between young children and adults. This underscores the importance of examining young children separately from all children in Census coverage analysis.

Data on trends for Black and Non-Black groups are provided in Chap. 4 as well. The importance of data on race and ethnicity is underscored by recent publications which document the many uses of Census Bureau's data on race and Hispanic Origin (The Leadership Conference Education Fund 2014; Prewitt 2014). However, the data available to study trends in undercounts by race is limited because historically there is only data on two groups (Blacks and Non-Black) and recent data has become more complex with the introduction of the more-than-one-race concept in official statistics. This issue is complex because of the fluidity of race as a social construct. For example, a recent analysis by the Census Bureau (Leibler et al. 2014) found almost ten million people who changed the way they identified themselves by race and/or Hispanic Origin status between the 2000 and the 2010 U.S. Decennial Census. The difficulty of providing meaningful and stable racial and ethnic categories for respondents underscores the important work currently underway at the Census Bureau (Krogstad 2014; U.S. Census Bureau 2013).

Data on the net undercount of young children at the state and county level are provided in Chap. 5. To study state and county undercounts of young children, Census results for those age 0–4 are compared to the Vintage 2010 Census Bureau's Population Estimates. This type of analysis is only legitimate for the population under age 10. Population Estimates for older groups are linked to the previous Census so the difference between the Population Estimates and the Census counts also reflect difference in Census coverage. As Chap. 5 underscores there are big differences in the net undercount experiences across states and counties and the evidence clearly indicates net undercounts for young children are concentrated in large counties, both in terms of numbers missed and high undercount rates.

A high net undercount of young children has been documented in societies as varied as China, South Africa, Laos and the former Soviet Union (Goodkind 2011; Anderson and Silver 1985; Anderson 2004). In Chap. 6, some of the data regarding the undercount of children in other countries are examined.

While there is a smattering of data documenting the high net Census undercount of young children, there has been almost no research on reasons for the high net undercount of this group. In Chap. 7, several ideas that might account for the high net undercount of young children are explored and where it exists, data are examined to assess these ideas. It is important to recognize the ideas must not just explain why children have a net undercount in the Decennial Census, they must explain why young children have a much higher net undercount rate than older children or adults.

The information in Chap. 7 should be is seen as a start to investigating the reasons behind the high net undercount of young children in the Census. More research is needed in this area. If we do not know the reasons young children are missed in the Census we are unlikely to find a remedy for the problem.

Chapter 8 provides a short summary of the main points of the book and offers a few comments on planning for the 2020 U.S. Decennial Census.

1.2 Intended Audience

This book provides information on the net undercount of young children in the Census from a variety of scattered sources. My main goals are to elevate the visibility of this issue and to provide future researchers with a foundation and a point of departure for studying the net undercount of young children.

The book is aimed at professionals in the scholarly world and selected "practitioners" outside of the scholarly world. The book will help round out the literature in demography and/or population studies courses and it can be used by professionals at the Census Bureau and related government organizations such as the U.S. General Accountability Office, The Congressional Research Service, and The U.S. Office of Management and Budget. Professional organizations that monitor the Census such as the Population Association of America, the American Statistical Association, and the non-profit organizations such as Population Reference Bureau, The Funders Census Initiative, and The Census Project may also find this publication useful.

Largely because of the social equity issues raised by the high net undercount of young children, the book may be of interest to some child advocacy organizations. Given the high level of net undercounts for Black (Alone or in Combination) and Hispanic young children, the book may be of interest to groups that represent the interests of these groups.

Evidence presented in Chap. 6 indicates that young children have relatively high net undercounts in many other countries, so the information in this book may be of interest to demographers and Census experts in other nations. Since young children are under-reported in some major surveys as well as the Census, this volume may also be of interest to the survey research field.

1.3 The Importance of Census Undercounts

To understand the importance of Census undercounts it is important to understand how Census data are used. In addition to our scientific and scholarly interest in obtaining correct Census counts, there are a number of practical and policy-related reasons why it is important to assess coverage in the Census. The high net undercount of young children is important because it is both a data problem and a social equity issue.

Perhaps the issue that brought more attention to Census undercounts than any other was the debate about making adjustments in Census figures for known undercounts. In the 1980, 1990 and 2000 Censuses, this was an ongoing topic of debate (Choldin 1994). In the 2000 Census, the Census Bureau was planning to make adjustments for undercounts, but in the end the Census Bureau decided that such adjustments should not be made based on technical grounds. Since the 2000 Census, the adjustment of Census figures to account for undercounts has not received much public attention.

It is important to recognize that sub-national Census undercounts and overcounts are critical in terms of public policy consequences. Although children can't vote, the demographic numbers from the Census are used to distribute political power both in terms of the constitutionally-mandated apportioning of seats in Congress to states based on population and in the judicially mandated one-person/one-vote rule used for constructing political districts from state legislative districts to city council and school board districts (Grofman 1982; McKay 1965; Balinski and Young 1982).

As mentioned earlier, state Census counts are used for apportioning the seats in the U.S. House of Representatives (Conk 1987) and sometimes small differences can be important. Crocker (2011) found that if the 2010 Census count for North Carolina had been 15,753 higher it would have received an additional seat in Congress. The analysis shown later in this book indicates there was a net undercount of about 25,000 children age 0–4 in North Carolina. Of course, if the young children had been counted more accurately in North Carolina, they probably would have been counted more accurately in other states as well, but this example shows how small miscounts might have large implications for political representation. The bottom line is any geographic area that is undercounted in the Census is not likely to get its fair share of political power (Anderson and Fienberg 2001; Bryant and Dunn 1995).

Census data are also used in many federal funding formulas that distribute more than $400 billion to states and localities each year (U.S. Senate 1992; Reamer 2010; Blumerman and Vidal 2009). Places that experience a net undercount do not receive their fair share of such public resources (PriceWaterhouseCoopers 2001). Table 1.1 shows four federal programs that distribute federal funds totaling nearly $20 billion in Fiscal Year 2013 based in part on the population age 0–4.

Chapter 5 shows that state net undercount rates for age 0–4 range from a net undercount of 10.2 % in Arizona to a net overcount of 2.1 % in North Dakota. States with relatively high net undercount rates (such as Arizona, California, Texas, and Florida) would likely benefit disproportionately in terms of receiving a larger share of federal funds if young children were counted more accurately in the 2020 Census.

The undercount of an age group in the Census also has implications for Population Estimates and Projections. The Census Bureau's Post-Census Population Estimates program (U.S. Census Bureau 2014a) uses data from the Census as the

Table 1.1 Four federal assistance programs using population age 0–5 in the distribution formula

	Fiscal year 2013 (in billions)
Special supplemental nutrition program for women, infants, and children (WIC program)	$6.5
Head start	$7.6
Child care and development block grant (mandatory plus discretionary)	$5.1
Maternal and child health services block grant to the states	$0.6
Total	$19.8

Source Reamer (2010) and First Focus (2014)

starting point to produce yearly Post-Census estimates. If an age cohort is under-counted in the Census, that cohort will be under-represented in the Census Bureau's Population Estimates for the next decade.

The 2010 Census figures are also used as the base for Census Bureau Population Projections, so undercounts in the Census are likely to be reflected in projections for many years (U.S. Census Bureau 2014b). State population projections, such as those available from the University of Virginia's Weldon Cooper Center for Public Service (2013), are also affected by Census undercounts. In discussing where to get baseline data for state and local projections Smith and colleagues (2001, p. 113) note, "The most commonly used source–and the most comprehensive in terms of demographic and geographic detail–is the Census of population and housing."

In addition, Census results and the Census Bureau's Population Estimates are often used to weight sample surveys both inside and outside government. If the Census counts and subsequent Population Estimates underestimate young children, the weighted survey results will reflect this error (O'Hare and Jensen 2014; O'Hare et al. 2013).

Some reports suggest that the net undercount of children leads to an under-estimation of poverty for this group (Daponte and Wolfson 2003; Hernandez and Denton 2001). Hernandez and Denton (2001, p. 1) conclude that the number of children in poverty in 1990 might have been as much as 2 million higher than what was reported because of the undercount of children in the Census.

Data from the Census counts as well as estimates and projections based on the Census are used for many planning activities including schools (Edmonston 2001). The high net undercounts of young children in many large urban counties (see Chap. 5) are likely to compromise school planning in those areas.

In addition, data from the Census Bureau are often used as denominators for constructing rates such as the child mortality rates. Census undercounts may skew such rates. For example, the U.S. death rate for all children age 1–4 in 2010 was 26.5 per 100,000 and for Hispanic children age 1–4 it was 22.7 per 100,000 (Murphy et al. 2013). These rates are based on using the Census counts as denominators. If one had used the DA estimates instead of the Census counts, the death rate for all children age 1–4 would have been 25.3 and the rate for Hispanic children age 1–4 would have been 20.9. This represents a 5 % difference for all children and an 8 % difference for Hispanic children.

West and Fein (1990) as well as Clogg and colleagues (1989) review several ways in which the Census undercounts affect social science research results. Clogg and his colleagues (1989, p. 559) conclude, "Because undercount rates (or coverage rates) vary by age, race, residence and other factors typically studied in social science research, important conceptual difficulties arise in using Census results to corroborate sampling frames or to validate survey results."

Moreover, high net undercounts of young children can provide misleading public impressions about the perceived size or growth of the population. This point is difficult to quantify but in many instances the size of a population translates into the perceived importance given to that population. In response to the 2000 Census, one public official stated "Pride in the community is involved. I want people to really know how big we are." (Cited in Prewitt 2003, p. 7). Since the net under-count of young children is concentrated geographically and racially, the impact of misperceptions is likely to be concentrated as well.

Finally, in order to improve Census-taking procedures in the future, it is impor-tant to understand which groups were undercounted at the highest rates in the 2010. As this manuscript is being written, the 2020 Census is about five years away. Given the size and complexity of the Census-taking operations, planning needs to be finalized in the next few years. This does not allow much time for the Census Bureau to determine what causes the high net undercount of young children and to test methodology to remedy the problem before plans for the 2020 Census need to be finalized.

References

Anderson, M., & Fienberg, S. E. (2001). *Who counts? The politics of census taking in contempo-rary America*. New York: Russell Sage Foundation.

Anderson, B. A. (2004). *Undercount in China's 2000 census in comparative perspective*. PSC Research Report, No. 04-565, Population Studies Center, University of Michigan, Ann Arbor, MI.

Anderson, B. A., & Silver, B. D. (1985). Estimating census undercount from school. *Demography, 22*(2), 289–308.

Balinski, M., & Young, H. P. (1982). *Fair representation: Meeting the ideal of one man, one vote*. New Haven, CT: Yale University Press.

Blumerman, L. M., & Vidal, P. M. (2009). *Uses of population and income statistics in federal funds distribution–with a focus on census bureau data*. Government Divisions Report Series, Research Report #2009-1, U.S. Census Bureau, Washington, DC.

Bryant, B. E., & Dunn, W. (1995). *Moving power and money: The politics of U.S. census taking*. Ithaca NY: New Strategists Publications.

Brick, J. M., & Williams, D. (2012). Explaining rising nonresponse rates in cross-sectional sur-veys. *The ANNALS of the American Academy of Political and Social Science, 645*, 36–59.

Choldin, H. M. (1994). *Looking for the last percent: The controversy over census undercounts*. New Jersey: Rutgers University Press.

Clogg, C. C., Massaglie, M. P., & Eliason, S. R. (1989). Population undercount and social sci-ence research. *Social Indicators Research, 21*(6), 559–598.

Conk, M. (1987). *According to their respective numbers*. New Haven, CT: Yale University Press.

Crocker, R. (2011). House apportionment 2010: States gaining, losing and on the margin. Congressional Research Service, 7-5700 R41584.

Daponte, B. O., & Wolfson, L. J. (2003). *How many American children are poor? Considering census undercounts by comparing census to administrative data*. Unpublished paper.

Darga, K. (1999). *Sampling and the census*. Washington DC: AEI Press.

Edmonton, B. (2001). *Effects of U.S. census undercoverage on analyses of school enrollments: A case study of Portland public schools*. U.S. Census Monitoring Board, Report Series, Report No. 5, February.

Fay, R. E., Passel, J. S., Robinson, J. G., & with Assistance from Cowan, C. D. (1988). *The coverage of the population in the 1980 census*. U.S. Census of Population and Housing, Evaluation and Research Reports, PHC80-E4, U.S Census Bureau, Washington, DC.

First Focus. (2014). *Children's budget: 2014*. Washington, DC: First Focus.

Goodkind, D. (2011). Child underreporting, fertility and sex ratio imbalance in China. *Demography, 48*, 291–316.

Griffin, D. H. (2014). Final task force report: Task force on the undercount of young children. Washington, DC: Memorandum for Frank A. Vitrano, U.S. Census Bureau.

Grofman, B. (1982). *Representation and redistricting issues*. Lexington, MA: Lexington Books.

Groves, R. (2010). *Children count too! Census bureau's directors blog March 9*. Washington, DC: U.S. Census Bureau.

Groves, R. M., & Couper, M. P. (1998). *Nonresponse in household interview surveys*. Hoboken: Wiley.

Hernandez, D., & Denton, N. (2001). *Census affects children in poverty*. Washington, DC: U.S. Census Monitoring Board.

Hillygus, D. S., Prewitt, K., & Pals, H. (2006). *The hard count: The political and social challenges of census mobilization*. New York: The Russell Sage Foundation.

Krogstad, J. M. (2014). *U.S. census looking at big changes in how it asks about race and ethnicity*. Washington, DC: Pew Research Center.

Leibler, C. A., Rastogi, S., Fernandez, L. E., Noon, J. M., & Ennis, S. R. (2014). *America's churning races: Race and ethnic response changes between census 2000 and the 2010 Census*, CARRA working paper series, working paper *#2014-09*. Center for Administrative Records Research and Applications. U.S. Census Bureau, Washington, DC.

Martin, E. (2007). Strength of attachment: survey coverage of people with tenuous ties to residences. *Demography, 44*(2), 437–440.

McKay, R. (1965). *Reapportionment: The law and politics of equal representation*. New York, NY: The Twentieth Century Fund.

Murphy, S. L., Xu, J., & Kochanek, K. D. (2013). *Deaths: Final data for 2010*. National Vital Statistics Reports, National Center for Health Statistics, 61(4), 1–117.

O'Hare, W. P. (1999). *The overlooked undercount: Children missed in the U.S. decennial census*. KIDS COUNT Working Paper, The Annie. E. Casey Foundation, Baltimore, MD.

O'Hare, W. P. (2009). *Why Are Young Children Missed So Often in the Census*. KIDS COUNT Working Paper, The Annie E. Casey Foundation, Baltimore, MD.

O'Hare, W. P., Jensen, E., & O'Hare, B. C. (2013). *Assessing the undercount of young children in the U.S. decennial census: Implications for survey research and potential explanations*. Paper presented at the 2013 American Association of Public Opinion Researchers Annual Conference, Boston, MA.

O'Hare, W. P. (2014a). Assessing net coverage error for young children in the 2010 U.S. decennial census. *Center for Survey Measurement Study Series (Survey Methodology #2014-02)*. U.S. Census Bureau.

O'Hare, W. P. (2014b). Historical examination of net coverage error for children in the U.S. decennial census: 1950 to 2010. *Center for Survey Measurement Study Series (Survey Methodology #2014-03)*. U.S. Census Bureau, Washington, DC.

O'Hare, W. P. (2014c). Assessing net coverage for young children in the 2010 U.S. decennial census. *International Journal of Population Research*, 2014, doi:10.1155/2014/671715.

O'Hare, W. P., & Jensen, E. B. (2014). *The representation of young children in the American community survey*. Presentation at the ACS Users Group Conference, Washington, DC. May 29–30.

Pitkin, J., & Park, J. (2005). The gap between births and U.S. census counts of children born in California: Undercount or transnational movement? Paper presented at the Population Association of America Conference, Philadelphia PA.

Prewitt, K. (2003). *Politics and science in census taking. The American People: Census 2000, Russell Sage Foundation and Population Reference Bureau*. Population Reference Bureau, Washington, DC.

Prewitt, K. (2014). *What is your race? The census and our flawed efforts to classify Americans*. Princeton, NJ: Princeton University Press.

PriceWaterhouseCooper. (2001). *Effect of U.S. decennial census 2000 undercount on federal funding to states and selected counties, 2001–2012*. Report to the U.S. Census Monitoring Board, Presidential Members.

Reamer, A. D. (2010). *Counting for dollars*. Brookings Institute, Metropolitan Policy Program, Washington, DC.

Robinson, G. J., Bashir, A., Das Dupta, P., & Woodward, K. A. (1993). Estimates of population coverage in the 1990 United States U.S. census based on demographic analysis. *Journal of the American Statistical Association, 88*(423), 1061–1071.

Robinson, G. J., & Adlaka, A. (2002). *Comparison of A.C.E. Revision II Results with Demographic Analysis*. DSSD A.C.E. Revision II Estimates Memorandum Series #PP-41, December 31, 2002, U.S. Census Bureau, Washington, DC.

Robinson, J. G. (2010). Coverage of population in census 2000 based on demographic analysis: The history behind the numbers. Population Division Working Paper N0. 91, U.S. Census Bureau, Washington, DC.

Skerry, P. (2000). *Counting on the census?*. Washington DC.: Brookings.

Smith, S., Tayman, J., & Swanson, D. A. (2001). *State and local population projections: Methods and analysis*. Kluwer: The Plenum Series on Demographic Methods and Population Analysis.

The Leadership Conference Education Fund/Advancing Justice/National Association of Latino Elected Officials (2014). *Race and ethnicity in the 2020 census: Improving data to capture a multiethnic America*. Leadership Conference Education Fund, Washington DC.

U.S. Senate. (1992). *Dividing dollars: Issues in adjusting decennial counts and intercensal estimates for funds distribution*. Report prepared by the Subcommittee on Government Information and Regulation of the Committee on Government Affairs, 102nd Congress, 2nd session Senate Print 102–83, U.S. Government Printing Office, Washington, DC.

U.S. Census Bureau. (1944). *Population differential fertility: 1940 and 1910; standardized fertility rates and reproduction rates*. Appendix A, Completeness of Enumeration of Children Under 5 Years Old in the U.S. Census of 1940 and 1910, 1940 Census, U.S. Census Bureau, Washington, DC.

U.S. Census Bureau. (1974). *Estimates of coverage of population by sex, race and age: demographic analysis*, 1970 U.S. Census of Population and Housing, Evaluation and Research Program, PHC (E)-4, U.S. Census Bureau, Washington, DC.

U.S. Census Bureau. (2012). *2010 Census coverage measurement estimation*. Report: Summary of Estimates of Coverage for Persons *in the* United States, DSSD 2010 Census Coverage Measurement Memorandum Series #2010-G-01, U.S. Census Bureau, Washington, DC.

U.S. Census Bureau. (2013). *2010 Census race and hispanic origin alternative questionnaire experiment*. 2010 Census Planning Memorandum Series, No. 211 (2nd reissue), U.S. Census Bureau, Washington, DC.

U.S. Census Bureau. (2014a). *The 2013 population estimates*. Washington, DC: U.S. Census Bureau.

U.S. Bureau of the Census. (2014b). U.S. population projections: 2014–2060. Release Number CB14-TPS.86, U.S. Census Bureau, Washington, DC.

Velkoff, V. (2011). *Demographic evaluation of the 2010 census*. Paper presented at the 2011 population association of America annual conference, Washington, DC.

Weldon Cooper Center for Public Service. (2013). Projections for the 50 States and D.C.

West, K. K., & Fein, D. J. (1990). U.S. Census undercount: An historical and contemporary sociological issues. *Sociological Inquiry, 60*(2), 127–141.

West, K., & Robinson, J. G. (1999). *What do we know about the undercount or children?* Population Division Working Paper, U.S. Census Bureau, Washington, DC.

Chapter 2
Methodology Used to Measure Census Coverage

Abstract The two primary methods used to assess the accuracy of the U.S. Census (Demographic Analysis and Dual Systems Estimates) are introduced. A short history of Demographic Analysis (DA) in assessing the U.S Census is presented. The methodologies for DA and Dual Systems Estimates are provided along with the potential errors and limitations in the DA method. The reasons why DA is the preferred method for assessing census coverage for young children are presented.

Keywords Demographic analysis · Dual systems estimates · Post enumeration survey · Census coverage measurement

How do we know who is missed in a Census? Several methods have been used over time and in various countries to answer this question but in the U.S. only the Demographic Analysis method and the Dual Systems Estimates method (sometimes called Post Enumeration Survey) provide quantitative answers to the question posed above (Mulry 2014; Hogan et al. 2013; Bryan 2004; Anderson 2004).

Demographic Analysis or (DA) has been used since the 1950s to provide estimates of net undercounts in the U.S. Census. This method creates a separate independent estimate of the expected population based largely on births and deaths which is compared to the Census counts.

The Dual System Estimates (DSE) method compares Census results to the results of a Post-Enumeration Survey to determine the number and characteristics of people who are omitted or included erroneously (mostly those double-counted).

Nomenclature can be confusing in this arena. The terms Dual Systems Estimates (DSE) and Post-Enumeration Survey (PES) are often used interchangeably. Sometimes the DSE or PES approach is simply called the "survey method." Moreover, the DSE/PES approach has been given a different name in each of the past three U.S. Censuses. In 2010 it was called Census Coverage Measurement (CCM), in the 2000 Census it was called Accuracy and Coverage Evaluation (A.C.E.) and in the 1990 Census it was called the Post Enumeration Survey (PES).

© The Author(s) 2015
W.P. O'Hare, *The Undercount of Young Children in the U.S. Decennial Census*,
SpringerBriefs in Population Studies, DOI 10.1007/978-3-319-18917-8_2

The analysis presented in this book rests largely on the results of the Census Bureau's Demographic Analysis (DA) method for assessing Census accuracy. I am convinced that DA is a better method for assessing the net undercount of young children because DA rests on highly accurate birth and death records and the least accurate component of DA, net international migration, is a very small component of DA Population Estimates for young children. The simplicity of the DA methodology relative to the DSE methodology can also be seen as an advantage. In addition, the DA data are advantageous because the data are available by single-year of age and consistent DA data are available from 1950 to 2010. The reasons for focusing on the results of Demographic Analysis rather than the U.S. Census Bureau's Dual System Estimates results are explored in more detail later in this Chapter.

2.1 Demographic Analysis History

The DA method has been used to assess the accuracy of Census figures for more than a half century and its origins are often traced back to an article by Price (1947). The unexpectedly high number of young men who turned up at the first compulsory selective service registration in October 1940, alerted scholars to the possibility of under-enumeration in the 1940 Decennial Census. The selective service data also provided an independent population estimate for assessing the size of such under-enumeration in the Decennial Census.

In one of the first systematic efforts to use DA to examine U.S. Census results, Coale (1955) found children age 0–4 had a relatively high net undercount rate in the Censuses of 1940 and 1950. Coale (1955, p. 35) used a variant of the Demographic Analysis technique to estimate net undercount rates for several population subgroups age 0–4 in 1950. In 1950, the estimated net undercount from Coale's analysis for age 0–4 ranged from a low of 3.8 % for White females to a high of 11 % for Non-White males. All of the estimates for the net undercount of age 0–4 were higher than the corresponding net undercount estimates for the total population.

Siegel and Zelnik (1966) found a substantial net undercount of children age 0–4 in the 1950 and 1960 Censuses. For the 1960 Census, their preferred composite estimate based on demographic analysis, indicated a net undercount of 2.0 % for White males age 0–4 and 1.2 % of White females age 0–4, 8.4 % for Non-White males and 6.8 % for Non-White females.

Coale and Zelnick (1963) found high net undercount rates for young children in the U.S. Census as far back as 1880, a finding supported by Hacker (2013) who shows that native-born White children age 0–4 had higher than average net undercount rates in each U.S. Census from 1850 to 1930. Over the 1850–1930 period, Hacker estimates the net undercount for native born White males age 0–4 varied from a low of 4.0 % in 1890 to a high of 15.2 % in 1850 and for native born White females the net undercount rates vary from a low of 4.1 % in 1890 to a high of 15.4 % in 1850. In every Census between 1850 and 1930, except 1890, the net undercount of native born Whites age 0–4 was higher than the overall average.

Coale and Rives (1973) also found very high net undercount rates for young Black children in every U.S. Census from 1880 to 1970. Estimates for the Black male population age 0–4 range from 28.5 % in 1890 to 7.4 % in 1960.

In addition to the demographic data presented above, genealogical research also shows a pattern of underreporting young children as far back as the 1850s (Adams and Kasakoff 1991).

2.2 Demographic Analysis Method

Since there are already several detailed descriptions of the DA methodology available, I will only review the method briefly here (Robinson 2010; Himes and Clogg 1992; U.S. Census Bureau 2010a).

DA is an example of the cohort-component method of population estimation meaning each component of population change (births, deaths and migration) is estimated for each birth cohort. The cohort-component method of Population Estimates is one of the most widely used techniques in population estimation (Bryan 2004).

The DA method employed for the 2010 Census used one technique to estimate the population under age 75 and another method to estimate the population age 75 and older (West 2012). Since this study focuses on children, only the method used for people age 0–74 is discussed here (people under age 1 are classified as age 0).

The 2010 DA estimates for the population age 0–74 are based on the compilation of historical estimates of the components of population change: Births (B), Deaths (D), and Net International Migration (NIM). The data and methodology for each of these components is described in separate background documents prepared for the development and release of the Census Bureau's 2010 DA estimates (Robinson 2010; Devine et al. 2010; Bhaskar et al. 2010).

As described by the Census Bureau (2010a) the DA Population Estimates for age 0–74 are derived from the basic demographic accounting Eq. (2.1) applied to each birth cohort:

$$P_{0-74} = B - D + NIM \qquad (2.1)$$

P_{0-74} Population for each single year of age from 0 to 74
B   Number of births for each age cohort
D   Number of deaths for each age cohort since birth
NIM   Net International Migration for each age cohort

For example, the estimate for the population age 17 on the April 1, 2010 Census date is based on births from April 1992 through March 1993, reduced by the deaths to that birth cohort in each year between 1992 and 2010, and incremented by Net International Migration (NIM) experienced by the cohort.

Births, deaths and Net International Migration detailed figures are not available for single year of age in the DA estimates released in May 2012 which is the

Table 2.1 Fundamental data for census Bureau's DA estimate for the population age 0–4

Births (in 5 years prior to the 2010 Census)	21,120,000
Deaths to those born in 5 years prior to Census	154,000
Net international migration	240,000
DA population estimate for age 0–4	21,206,000
Population age 0–4 counted in 2010 Census	20,201,000

Source U.S. Census Bureau (2010b)

primary source of DA data used here. But the December 2010 DA "Middle Series" estimate for the population age 0 to 4 is comprised of 21,120,000 births, 154,000 deaths, and Net International Migration of 240,000 (see Table 2.1). Births are by far the largest component of the DA Population Estimates for young children. In 2010, births accounted for 99.6 % of the DA population estimate for the population age 0–4 (U.S. Census Bureau 2010b).

The birth and death data used in the Census Bureau's DA estimates come from the U.S. National Center on Health Statistics (NCHS) and these records are widely viewed as being accurate and complete. The National Center for Health Statistics (2014, p. 2) states, "A chief advantage of birth certificate data is that information is collected for essentially every birth occurring in the country each year..." After a thorough review of vital statistics prior to the 2010 Census, the Census Bureau (Devine et al. 2010, p. 5) stated:

> The following assumptions are made regarding the use of vital statistics for DA:
> - Birth registration has been 100 % complete since 1985.
> - Infant deaths were underregistered at one-half the rate of the underregistration of births up to and including 1959.
> - The registration of deaths for ages 1 and over has been 100 % complete for the entire DA time series starting in 1935.

Although some of the characteristics gathered on birth certificates may be suspect, the number of births and deaths is widely seen as virtually complete.

In addition to regularly published totals, the Census Bureau receives microdata files from NCHS containing detailed monthly data on each birth and death. These files were used for DA estimates by race. Construction of DA estimates by race is discussed later in this Chapter.

The Census Bureau changed the way it calculated Net International Migration for the 2010 set of DA estimates (Bhaskar et al. 2010). The current method relies heavily on data from the Census Bureau's American Community Survey (ACS) where the location of the Residence One Year Ago (ROYA) is ascertained for everyone in the survey age 1 or older. The total number of yearly immigrants is derived from this question in each year of the ACS, and then that total number of immigrants is distributed to demographic cells (sex, age and race) based on an accumulation of the same data over the last 5 years of the ACS. Five years of ACS data are used to provide more stable and reliable estimates for small demographic groups. On the other hand, we should note that the five-year average may mask changes over time. Given changing economic conditions, it would not be surprising if the immigration pattern in the 2008–2010 period differed from the pattern before 2008, however, I suspect such errors would be small, especially for those age 0–4. NIM is available by single year of age for Blacks (Black Alone and Black Alone or in Combination) under age 30 and for Hispanics under age 20.

Statistics on emigration of the foreign-born population from the U.S. are based on a residual method comparing data on the foreign-born population from the 2000 Census to later ACS estimates to develop rates and then applying those rates to observed populations (Demographic Analysis Research Team 2010).

Emigration of U.S. citizens (net native migration) is derived by examining Census data from several other countries (Schachter 2008). This method of estimating out migration is problematic for a couple of reasons. Data are not available for every country and the quality of some foreign Censuses is suspect. However, with few exceptions (see Pitkin and Park 2005) it is widely felt that such emigration has little impact on DA Estimates for young children.

The DA estimates released in May 2012 assume a Net International Migration of only 244,000 out of a population of 21,172,000 for age 0–4 (the 244,000 figure was obtained from Census Bureau staff). Thus Net International Migration accounts for only 1.1 % of the DA estimate for the population age 0–4. Since Net International Migration accounts for such a small part of the DA estimate for the population age 0–4, errors in this component of population change would not have a big impact on the final DA population estimate for the 0–4 age group. In addition, potential errors in the overall estimates of the DA estimates for the population age 0–4 are likely to be small, as discussed below.

In preparing for the December 2010 DA release, the Census Bureau developed five estimation series with differing assumptions to reflect the degree of uncertainty in the estimates. For the population age 0–17, the estimates from the five series presented in December 2010 range from 75,042,000 to 76,222,000 and for the population age 0–4 the estimates ranged from 21,181,000 to 21,265,000. This is a relatively small band of uncertainty compared to the estimated net undercount.

The assumptions about births and deaths were the same for each of the five series. Only the assumptions about Net International Migration varied. In those five series the Net International Migration assumptions for the population age 0 to 4 ranged from 214,000 to 297,000 (U.S. Census Bureau 2010b). The Middle Series estimate of net immigration for age 0–4 was 240,000 for the DA estimates released in December 2010. Thus the high end of the immigration assumption was 57,000 persons higher than the Middle Series and the low end was 26,000 persons lower than the Middle Series.

This provides some guidance about the size of potential errors in immigration estimates and population estimates used in DA for young children. If the Net International Migration component for children age 0–4 in the DA estimate from May 2012 had been 26,000 less, the net undercount of children age 0–4 in the 2010 Census would be 4.5 % instead of the value of 4.6 % reported in the May 2012 DA release. If the Net International Migration component for children age 0–4 had been 57,000 higher the net undercount estimates would have been 4.9 %. In either case, the net undercount of young children would remain much higher than any other age group. If one wanted to look at an extreme case and assume there was no net immigration of children age 0–4, the DA estimate for the net undercount of the population age 0–4 would 3.6 %, which is still much higher than for any other age group.

For older children, Net International Migration plays a bigger role. For the population age 14–17 the May 2012 DA shows a net overcount of 1.4 %. For the population age 14–17, the Net International Migration assumptions for the five DA series released in December 2010, range from 1.023 million for the low series to 1.424 million in the high series and compose 6.1 and 8.3 % of the DA estimate respectively. The Net International Migration assumption for the December 2010 DA Middle Series was 1.186 million. Thus the high end of the series was 238,000 persons higher than the Middle Series estimate and the low end of the series was 163,000 lower than the Middle Series. If the DA estimate for the population age 14–17 were 238,000 higher than the May 2010 Middle Series, it would result in an overcount estimate of essentially zero. If the DA estimate for the population age 14–17 were 163,000 lower than the May 2012 Middle Series, it would result in an overcount estimate of 2.4 %.

2.3 Limitations of the Demographic Analysis Method

There are four major limitations to DA. First, it is only routinely available for the nation as a whole. The population age 0–9 is an exception to this rule. Sub-national analysis can be done for the population under age ten, because the Census Bureau's Population Estimates for age 0–9 are not linked to the previous Census. This issue is explored in Chap. 5.

Second, DA estimates are only available for a few race/ethnic groups. Historically the estimates have only been available for Black and Non-Black groups. This restriction is due to the lack of race specificity and consistency for data collected on the birth and death certificates historically. The only group that has been identified relatively consistently over time is Blacks (African-Americans).

The 2010 DA estimates include data for Hispanics for the first time, but only for the population under age 20. Hispanics under age 20 were included in the DA estimates in 2010 because Hispanics have been consistently identified in birth and death certificates since 1990.

The 2010 DA is the first to produce estimates of net undercount of Black Alone and Black Alone or in Combination. Recent changes in how the Census Bureau collects data on race raises questions about the comparability of the data for Blacks in the 2010 Census relative to earlier Censuses. This issue is explored in Chap. 4.

The third limitation of the DA estimates is that they only provide net under-count/overcount figures. A zero net undercount could be the result of no one being missed (omissions) or double counted (erroneous enumerations) or it could be the result of 10 % of the population being missed and 10 % double counted.

The fourth limitation of the DA methodology is the lack of any measures of uncertainty for the estimates similar to standard errors associated with surveys.

However, as mentioned earlier in this Chapter, in the December 2010 DA release, the Census Bureau released five different estimate series based on five sets of assumptions about births, deaths, and Net International Migration to reflect some of the uncertainty regarding the DA estimates.

Despite these limitations, DA has been used for many decades, the underlying data and methodology are strong, and it has provided useful information for those trying to understand the strengths and weaknesses of the U.S. Decennial Census. According to Robinson (2000, p. 1) "The national DA estimates have become the accepted benchmark for tracking historical trends in net Census undercounts and for assessing coverage differences by age, sex, and race (Black, all other)."

As stated earlier, DA is particularly useful for assessing the accuracy of the Census count of young children for two reasons. One of the major uncertainties in using DA to assess the accuracy of total population counts is the assumptions about Net International Migration that must be made. For most age groups other than young children, Net International Migration is subject to more error because of the greater uncertainty of some specific elements such as undocumented immigrants and uncertainty in the estimation of emigrants (Jensen 2012). According to Bhaskar and colleagues (2010, p. 1), "The largest uncertainty in the Demographic Analysis (DA) estimates comes from the international migration component." For young children, net international immigration is a very small factor, so any errors in the net immigration estimate will have little impact on the DA estimate for this age group.

The second reason DA is the preferred method for assessing the net under-count of young children is improved quality of vital events data. For people born in the United States in the past couple of decade's vital event data are deemed to be complete. In the five DA scenarios provided in the 2010 DA estimates released in December 2010, the birth and death assumptions are identical for people under age 18 in all five series, which reflects the high level of credibility given to the vital events data for children.

2.4 Dual Systems Estimates Methodology

The other major source of data on undercounts and overcounts in the U.S. Census is the Census Bureau's Dual Systems Estimates (DSE) method. The DSE approach for 2010 is called Census Coverage Measurement. This is an oversimplification, but basically DSE compares results from a Post-Enumeration Survey (PES) to Census records to determine undercounts and overcounts (Mule 2010). The 2010 Census is the first one where DSE has produced data for the population age 0–4, so there is no historical data on young children from DSE. In the 2000 U.S. Decennial Census, DSE estimates were made for age 0–9 and age 10–17, and in the 1990 Census DSE estimates for children were only available for the entire group of children age 0–17.

Table 2.2 shows differences between net undercount estimates of DA and DSE in the 2010 Census for several age groups. For all adult age groups examined, the

Table 2.2 Comparison of DA and DSE undercount estimates for several demographic groups: 2010

	DSE	DA	Difference (DA–DSE)
Age 0–4	0.7	4.6	−3.9
Age 5–9	−0.3	2.2	−2.5
Age 10–17	−1.0	−0.5	−0.5
Age 18-29 males	1.2	−0.4	1.6
Age 18-29 females	−0.3	−1.5	1.2
Age 30–49 males	3.6	2.3	1.3
Age 30–49 females	−0.4	−1.9	1.5
Age 50 + males	−0.3	0.5	0.1
Age 50 + females	−2.4	−2.4	0.1

Source O'Hare et al. (2012)

differences are less than 2 % points. However for the population age 0 to 4, the difference is 3.9 % points.

As noted above, for many age groups the DA method and the DSE method produce similar results. However, in the context of comparing the results of DSE and DA in the 2000 Census, and noting the generally consistent results, the U.S. Census Bureau (2003, p. v) observed,

> The primary exception to the consistency of results occurs for children aged 0-9. While the A.C.E. Revision II estimates a small net overcount for children 0-9 (the estimate was not statistically significantly different from zero), Demographic Analysis estimated a net undercount of 2.56 %. The Demographic Analysis estimate for this age group is more accurate than those for other age groups because the estimate for young children depends primarily on recent birth registration data which are believed to be highly accurate.

A National Research Council report (2004, p. 254) made the same observation about the inconsistency of DA and DSE estimates for young children and the authors note, "No explanation for this discrepancy has been advanced."

Table 2.3 shows the results of DA and DSE estimates of Census coverage for children in the 1990, 2000 and 2010 Censuses. The data indicate significant inconsistencies between the results of the two methodologies for young children. In 2010, the DSE estimated a 0.7 % net undercount for age 0–4 compared to 4.6 % for DA. In population terms, the 2010 DA estimates a net undercount of 970,000 people age 0–4, while the DSE estimated a net undercount of only 152,000 people in this age group.

Table 2.3 shows that in 2000 and 2010, the DA and DSE coverage estimates for age 10–17, are relatively consistent, but estimates for age 0–9 are different.

Table 2.3 Comparison of estimated net percent undercount from DA and DSE for population age 0–17 in 1990, 2000 and 2010

	1990		2000		2010	
	DA	DSE	DA	DSE	DA	DSE
Age 0–17	−1.8	−3.2	−0.7	0.8	1.7	0.3
Age 10–17			−1.8	−1.3	−0.5	−1.0
Age 0–9			−2.6	0.5	−3.4	−0.2
Age 0–4					−4.6	−0.7

Source O'Hare et al. (2012)

The 2000 DSE estimates for age 0–9 was +0.5 % compared to −2.6 % or DA. In 2010 the DSE coverage estimates for age 0–9 was −0.2 % compared to −3.4 % for DA.

It should be noted that in the 1990 Census the results of DSE showed a higher net undercount for all children age 0–17 than DA (3.2 % undercount from the DSE method compared to a 1.8 % undercount for the DA method). However, there was no disaggregation of the DSE data for children into smaller age groups. Given the very different net undercount rates for children in different age groups the implications of the 1990 data are not clear.

O'Hare and his colleagues (2012) provide detailed documentation of the inconsistency between DSE and DA estimates for young children and suggest that uncorrected correlation bias may result in an underestimation of the undercount for young children in the DSE methodology. The U.S Census Bureau (2012b p. 1) describes correlation bias as,

> Correlation bias results from the failure of the general independence assumption underlying dual system estimation. This form of bias tends to lead to underestimation of dual system estimates if persons missed in the Census are more likely than those found in the Census to also have been missed in the Census Coverage Measurement survey.

The issue of correlation bias in the DSE approach has been discussed by other researchers (Wachter and Freedman 1999; Shores 2002; Shores and Sands 2003). The National Research Council (2009) created a panel to study the issue of correlation bias and coverage measurement in the 2010 Census, but did not seem to take up the issue of correlation bias for young children in their deliberations.

The existence of correlation bias in the DSE method is already recognized for the adult Black male population. Currently, adjustments in the DSE estimates for adult Black males are made to correct for correlation bias (U.S. Census Bureau 2012b). No similar adjustments are made for young children, in part, because there is not a widely accepted method for doing so.

Another issue with the DSE method is the matching that is required to link records from the Census to the records in the Post Enumeration Survey. To oversimplify the situation, to use the DSE method, one must make a decision about whether a person named Jon Smith in the PES is the same as the person named Johnathan Smith in the Census. Of course there are usually other clues like age, sex and address to use in matching. Matching procedures have improved over time but this is still an area were potential errors may occur. It would be useful to know if matching is more difficult for young children.

The DSE method also depends on respondent recall and that introduces another potential problem. The Post Enumeration Survey is usually conducted 4–6 months after the April 1, Census date. In discussing residential location at the time of the Census, Martin (2007, p. 429) notes, "Respondents interviewed months after April 1 may find it difficult to recall accurately when a move occurred." Recall may be potential problem for other data as well.

In the absence of any other reason for the large difference in net undercount estimates for young children between the DA method and the DSE method, uncorrected correlation bias in the DSE method is the leading explanation for the observed differences. The Census Bureau Task Force on the Undercount of Young Children, (Griffin 2014, p. i) concluded, "The task force believes that Demographic Analysis (DA) provides the best measure of this undercount in the 2010 Census at 4.6 % nationally."

The strength of the DA method for assessing net undercounts in young children is widely recognized. In comparing the DA results to DSE results in the 2000 Decennial Census, Zeller (2006, p. 320) concluded, "Since the Demographic Analysis estimate for young children depended on highly accurate recent birth registration data, the Demographic Analysis estimate is believed to be more accurate. "Hogan and colleagues (2013, p. 98) also find, "Given the methodology that underlies DA, its estimates of younger populations tend to be quite accurate." In comparing the results of the Dual Systems Estimates and DA from the 2000 Census, Shores and Sands (2003, p. 10) conclude, "Demographic Analysis has the advantage that its estimates are constructed from administrative data sources, some of which (e.g. birth and death registration data) are quite accurate."

In the analysis shown in this publication, I rely almost exclusively on DA estimates. I believe the strengths of DA methodology make it a particularly good technique for estimating the number of young children. Moreover, in the decade prior to the 2010 Census, staff at the Census Bureau investigated a number of issues related to the production of DA estimates (Robinson 2010; Divine et al. 2010; Bhaskar et al. 2010). The increased input, review and examination enhance the likelihood that the 2010 DA estimates are accurate and credible.

In the remainder of this publication, the differences between the Census counts and DA estimates are shown as the Census count *minus* the DA estimate. This is consistent with the convention used by Velkoff (2011) in reporting the first results of the 2010 DA. This calculation is sometimes labeled "net Census coverage error" in other research. A negative number implies a net undercount and a positive number implies a net overcount. This may be a point of confusion because some studies have used a net undercount rate which subtracts the Census counts from the DA (or DSE) estimates. In that construction, a negative figure implies an overcount. I chose to use the net Census coverage error construction because I feel having an undercount reflected by a negative number is more intuitive. When figures are stated in the text as an undercount or an overcount, the positive and negative signs are not used.

In converting the differences between Census counts and DA estimates to percentages, the difference is divided by the DA estimate. Population Estimates are shown rounded to the nearest thousand for readability.

2.5 Measuring the Net Undercount of Children by Race

Black is the only race group that has been coded relatively consistently in birth and death certificate data over time, so the only groups for which DA estimates could be produced were Black and Non-Black.

Key to the DA method for Blacks and Non-Blacks is making the vital events data and the Census data consistent. There have always been issues in trying to make information from these two data systems consistent, but the challenge of making accurate DA estimates for Blacks and Non-Blacks has increased in recent years since respondents have been allowed to select more than one race. In discussing the use of vital statistics for DA estimates by race the Census Bureau (Devine et al. 2010, p. 4) concludes, "...developing the estimates for DA race categories comes with a more complex, and substantial set of challenges." See Robinson (2010) for a good general discussion of issues associated with racial classifications in the Census and the vital events registers.

There are multiple problems in trying to make data collected in the Census racial categories comparable to the race data collected on birth and death certificates. For example, the "Some Other Race" category is a response category for the race question in the Census but not in birth or death certificates. Because the birth certificate data do not have a "Some Other Race" category, the Census Bureau constructs a set of modified race categories from the Census responses in which respondents in the Some Other Race category are distributed to Black and Non-Black categories. Thus for making comparisons between DA estimates and the Census counts for Blacks and Non-Blacks, one must use the 2010 U.S. Census modified race tabulations available on the Census Bureau's website. Correctly re-assigning people from the "Some Other Race" category to Black and Non-Black categories is a challenge and provides a potential source of errors.

Another issue is the fact that Census respondents in 2000 and 2010 could mark more than one race. In 1997, the U.S. Office of Management and Budget (1997) updated Statistical Policy Directive 15 requiring federal data collection efforts to allow respondents to mark more than one race. Prior to the 2000 Census, respondents were only allowed to mark one race in the U.S. Decennial Census, which meant the race data from the U.S. Census and from vital events were consistent in this regard.

Another issue is that birth certificate forms only record the race of the mother and father while the race of a child is asked directly in the Decennial Census. Thus, for birth certificate data, the race of the newborn must be inferred from the race of the parent(s). This is further complicated by a significant level of missing data. While data on the race of mother is relatively complete, many birth certificates are missing data on the race of the father. In 2009, 19 % of birth certificate forms did not contain the race of the father (Martin et al. 2011).

When both parents report the same race, that race is assigned to the child. When the two parents report different races on the birth certificate, the Census Bureau assigns newborns to one of thirty-one race categories based on the reported race of their mother and father and on empirical parent-child race relationships seen in the 2000 and 2010 Census data (Ortman et al. 2012).

This issue is further complicated by the fact that is wasn't until 2003 that the federal government issued new standard birth certificate and death certificate forms allowing parents to mark more than one race. However, birth and death certificate data are collected by states and the states only adopted the new forms slowly over time. Every year after 2003, a new group of states adopted the new birth certificate and death certificate forms. Therefore, each year from 2003 to 2010 the Census Bureau received files on births from NCHS with two kinds of racial categories; one file where respondents were allowed to report multiple race data and one file where they were not. By 2010, 35 states and the District of Columbia were using the new federal birth and death certificate forms.

DA analysis requires that the mixed race data from the birth (and death) certificates be categorized as Black or Non-Black, based on both single-race and multiple-race reported by mother and fathers. For the 2010 DA estimates data from birth certificates were used to categorize people into Black Alone or Black Alone or in Combination categories. NCHS provided the Census Bureau with both the multiple races that are reported and the multiple race response "bridged" to the pre-1997 OMB single race categories. Details about the bridging method are provided by NCHS on their website.

Assignment of race on death certificates is also a potential problem but deaths contribute very little to the DA estimates for young children (Aries 2008).

Given the issues described above, one should view DA estimates for Blacks (Alone or Alone or in Combination) cautiously. Small differences or small changes over time could be due to methodological issues rather than real differences or changes.

The 2010 Census DA estimates were first released in December 2010 but in May 2012 the Census Bureau issued revised Demographic Analysis estimates, for the total population, the Black Alone population, the Black Alone or in Combination population, the Not Black Alone population and the Not Black Alone or in Combination population, but not for the Hispanic population (U.S. Census Bureau 2012a). The estimates for the Black Alone or in Combination populations were only provided for the population below age 30. The May 2012 DA estimates were based on the more recent birth and death data and improvements from ongoing research compared to the DA estimates originally released in December 2010. Since the DA estimate for Hispanics were not updated in the May 2012 release, I use the Middle Series of the December 2010 release for that group in my analysis.

2.6 Summary

The main methods for measuring coverage in the U.S. Census are Demographic Analysis (DA) and Dual Systems Estimates (DSE). These two methods produce results that are fairly consistent for all age groups except young children. For the population age 0–4, the DA method estimates a net undercount of 4.6 % compared to 0.7 % for the DSE method (the DSE method is called Census Coverage Measurement in the 2010 Census).

The DA method is widely viewed as the better method for estimating net undercount of young children because it relies heavily on vital events data which are very high quality and the most problematic component of DA, Net International

Migration, is only a very small part of the DA estimates for young children. Moreover, the undercount estimates for young children produced by DSE may suffer from correlation bias which results in an underestimates of the net undercount.

Given the challenges and complications to making the racial categories from the birth certificates consistent with those offered in the Census, net undercount estimates of the Black population should be used cautiously.

References

Adams, J. W., & Kasakoff, A. B. (1991). Estimates of U.S. decennial census underenumeration based on genealogies. *Social Science History, 15*(4), 527–543.

Anderson, B. A. (2004). *Undercount in China's 2000 census in comparative perspective*. PSC Research Report, No. 04-565, Population Studies Center, Ann Arbor, MI: University of Michigan.

Aries, E., Schauman W. S., Eschbach K., Sorlie P. D., & Backlund E. (2008).*The validity of race and hispanic origin reporting on death certificates in the United States* (Vol. 148, 2). Hyattsville: National Center for Health Statistics, Vital Health Statistics.

Bhaskar, R., Scopilliti, M., Hollman, F., & Armstrong, D. (2010). Plans for producing estimates of net international migration for the 2010 demographic analysis estimates. Census Bureau Working Paper No. 90.

Bryan, T. (2004). Population estimates. In J Siegel & D Swanson (Eds.), *The methods and materials of demography* (2nd ed.) Elsevier Academic Press, pp. 523–560.

Coale, A. J. (1955). The population of the United States in 1950 classified by age, sex and color-a revision of census figures. *Journal of the American Statistical Association, 50*, 16–54.

Coale, A. J., & Rives, N. W. (1973). A statistical reconstruction of black population of the United States: 1880 to 1970: Estimates of true numbers by age and sex, birth rates, and total fertility. *Population Index, 39*(1), 3–36.

Coale, A. J., & Zelnick, M. (1963). *New estimates of fertility and population in the United States*. Princeton NJ: Princeton University Press.

Demographic Analysis Research Team. (2010). *Estimates of net international migration in demographic analysis*. Population Division, U.S. Census Bureau, presentation at 2010 Demographic Analysis Conference, Washington DC, December 6.

Devine, J., Sink, L., DeSalvo, B., & Cortes R. (2010). *The use of vital statistics in the 2010 demographic analysis estimates*. Census Bureau Working Paper No. 88.

Griffin, D. H. (2014). Final task force report: Task force on the undercount of young children. *Memorandum for Frank A. Vitrano*. Washington, DC:U.S. Census Bureau, February 2.

Hacker, J. D. (2013). New estimates of census coverage in the United States: 1850–1930. *Social Science History, 37*(1), 71–101.

Himes, C. L., & Clogg, C. C. (1992). An overview of demographic analysis as a method for evaluating census coverage in the United States. *Population Index, 58*(4), 587–607.

Hogan, H., Cantwell, P., Devine, J., Mule, V. T., & Velkoff, V. (2013). Quality and the 2010 census. *Population Research and Public Policy, 32*, 637–662.

Jensen, E. (2012). *International migration and age-specific sex ratios in the 2010 demographic analysis*. Paper presented at the Applied Demography Conference at the University of Texas at San Antonio Texas, January.

Martin, E. (2007). Strength of attachment: Survey coverage of people with tenuous ties to residences. *Demography, 44*(2), 437–440.

Martin, J. A., Hamilton, B. E., & Ventura, S. J. (2011). *Births: final data for 2009, National Vital Statistics System* (Vol. 60, no. 1). Hyattsville, MD; National Center for Health Statistics.

Mule, V. T. Jr. (2010). *U.S. coverage measurement survey plans*. Paper delivered at the Joint Statistical Meetings, Vancouver, Canada.

Mulry, M. (2014). Measuring undercounts for hard-to-reach groups. In R. Tourangeau, B. Edwards, T. P. Johnson, K. M. Wolter, & N. Bates (Eds.), *Hard-to-survey populations*. Cambridge: Cambridge University Press.

National Center for Health Statistics. (2014). *Assessing the quality of medical and health data from the 2003 Birth certificate revision*: results from two states (Vol. 62, no. 2). National Vital Statistics Reports. U.S. Department of Health and Human Services, Centers for Disease Control and Prevention.

National Research Council. (2004). The 2000 census: Counting under adversity, panel to review the 2000 census. In C. F. Citro, D. L. Cork & J. L. Norwood (Eds.), *Committee on national statistics, division of behavioral and social science and education*. The National Academy Press, Washing DC, Page 254.

National Research Council. (2009). Coverage measurement in the 2010 census. In R. M. Bell & M. Cohen (Eds.), *Panel on correlation bias and coverage measurement in the 2010 decennial census*. Committee on National Statistics, Division of Behavioral and Social Sciences and Education, Washington, DC: National Academy Press.

O'Hare, W. P., Robinson, J. G., West, K., & Mule, T. (2012). *Comparing demographic analysis and dual-systems estimates results for children*. Paper presented at the Southern Demographic Association Conference, Williamsburg VA, October 11–12.

Ortman, J. M., Hollman, F. W., & Guarneri, C. E. (2012). *Measuring multiple-race births in the United States*. Presented at the Annual Meeting of the Population Association of America, San Francisco, CA: May 3–5, 2012.

Pitkin, J., & Park, J. (2005). *The gap between births and census counts of children born in California: Undercount or transnational movement?* Paper presented at the Population Association of America Conference, Philadelphia PA. March.

Price, D. O. (1947). A check on the underenumeration in the 1940 census. *American Sociological Review, 12*, 44–49.

Robinson, J. G. (2000). *Accuracy and coverage evaluation: Demographic analysis results*. U.S. Census Bureau, DSSD Census 2000 procedures for operations Memorandum Series B-4, U.S. Census Bureau. Page 1.

Robinson, J. G. (2010). *Coverage of population in census 2000 based on demographic analysis: The history behind the numbers*. U.S. Census Bureau, Working Paper No. 91.

Schachter, J. (2008). Estimating native emigration from the United States. Memorandum date December 24, delivered to the U.S .Census Bureau.

Shores, R. (2002). Accuracy and coverage evaluation revision ii adjustment for correlation bias. DSSD, A.C.E. REVISION II MEMORANDUM SERIES PP-53, U.S. Bureau of the Census, Dec.

Shores, R., & Sands, R. (2003) Correlation bias estimation in the accuracy and coverage evaluation revision II. In *Proceedings of the Survey Research methods Section, Joint Statistical Meetings*.

Siegel, J. S., & Zelnik, M. (1966). An evaluation of coverage in the 1960 U.S. census of population by techniques of demographic analysis and by composite methods. In *Proceedings of the Social Statistics Section of the American Statistical Association*: (1966): 71–85. Washington, D.C.: American Statistical Association.

U.S. Census Bureau. (2003). *Technical assessment of A.C.E. revision II*. Washington, DC: U.S. Census Bureau.

U.S. Census Bureau. (2010a). *The development and sensitivity analysis of the 2010 demographic analysis estimates*. Population Division Background paper of DA Conference Dec 6, 2010. 11/29/2010, Table 2, U.S. Census Bureau, Washington, DC.

U.S. Census Bureau. (2010b). Tables released at December 2010 conference.

U.S. Census Bureau. (2012a). Documentation for the revised 2010 demographic analysis middle series estimates. U.S. Census Bureau, Washington, DC.

U.S. Census Bureau. (2012b). *DSSD 2010 census coverage measurement memorandum series #2010-G-11*. 2010 Census Coverage Measurement Estimation Reports: Adjustment for Correlation Bias, U.S. Bureau of the Census, Washington, DC.

U.S. Office of Management and Budget. (1997). *Revisions to the standards for the classification of federal data on race and ethnicity*. Statistical Policy Directive 15, Federal Register Notice, October 30.

Velkoff, V. (2011). *Demographic evaluation of the 2010 census*. Paper presented at the 2011 PAA annual Conference, Washington, DC.

Wachter, K.W., & Freedman, D. A. (1999). The fifth cell: correlation bias in U.S. census adjustment. Technical Report Number 570. Berkeley: Department of Statistics, University of California.

West, K. (2012). *Using medicare enrollment file for the DA 2010 estimates*. Paper presented at the Applied Demography Conference at the University of Texas at San Antonio Texas, January.

Zeller, A. (2006). *Inconsistency between accuracy and coverage evaluation revision II and demographic analysis estimates for children 0 to 9 years of age*. Paper presented at the American Statistical Association annual conference.

Chapter 3
Coverage of Young Children in the 2010 U.S. Decennial Census

Abstract For the total population there was a small net undercount in the 2010 U.S. Census but this is a product of a 1.7 % net under count for children (age 0–17) an a 0.7 % net overcount for adults (age 18 plus). Demographic Analysis (DA) shows young children (age 0–4) had a higher net undercount than any other age group in the 2010 U.S. Census and that younger children had higher net undercount rates than older children. Young Blacks Alone or in Combination and Hispanics had higher net undercount rates than others.

Keywords Census coverage · Net undercount · Undercount differentials · Children · Young children

This Chapter focuses on net coverage for children in the 2010 U.S. Decennial Census. The next Chapter will look at the results of the 2010 Census compared to historical data on the net undercount of young children.

As in the past, the DA program for 2010 produced estimates by age, sex, and race. However, the 2010 DA analysis included three new facets. For the first time, the Census Bureau provided DA estimates for the Hispanic population under age 20. Secondly, for the first time the Census Bureau published DA estimates of the Black Alone and the Black Alone or in Combination populations for those under age 30. Third, in order to reflect some of the uncertainty in the DA estimates, the Census Bureau produced five sets of estimates based on different assumptions about vital events and Net International Migration for the DA estimates released in December 2010 (U.S. Census Bureau 2010). It is also noteworthy that unlike the past several Censuses there was no report based on DA from the Census Bureau following the 2010 Census. Only the file with the underlying data was made available.

This chapter draws heavily from a Working Paper available on the U.S. Census Bureau's website (O'Hare 2014a) and a related journal article (O'Hare 2014b).

W.P. O'Hare, *The Undercount of Young Children in the U.S. Decennial Census*,
SpringerBriefs in Population Studies, DOI 10.1007/978-3-319-18917-8_3

Initially the Census Bureau released their DA estimates for 2010 in early December of 2010 in an effort to publish the DA estimates before the 2010 Census results were released. This was done to try and mitigate perceptions that the DA results were influenced by the Census count which was not released until late December 2010 (U.S. Census Bureau 2010). In May 2012, the Census Bureau issued revised Demographic Analysis estimates, for the total population, the Black Alone population, the Black Alone or in Combination population, the Not Black Alone population and the Not Black Alone or in Combination population (U.S. Census Bureau 2012). It should be noted, however, that the revised DA estimates issued in May 2012 were only for the Middle Series of the five alternatives released in December 2010 and did not include an update of DA estimates for Hispanics. Because no Hispanic DA estimates were provided in the May 2012 release, data for Hispanics used in this analysis are taken from the Middle Series of Census Bureau's DA estimates issued in December 2010. All other data are from the May 2012 DA release.

3.1 2010 Demographic Analysis Results by Age

In the 2010 Census there was a net overcount of 0.1 % of the total population based on DA, which translates into about 400,000 people (Velkoff 2011). However, the small net overcount for the total population masks important differences among some age groups.

Velkoff (2011) shows the 0.1 % net overcount for the entire population is a product of a 0.7 % net overcount for adults (age 18 an older) and a 1.7 % net undercount for children (age 0–17). In population numbers, these reflect a net undercount of 1.3 million children and a net overcount of 1.7 million adults. This underscores the extent to which the small difference between the 2010 Census and the DA estimates for the total population conceals important differences by age.

Figure 3.1 shows the net undercount and overcount figures from the 2010 Census by single year of age for ages 0–84. The age-specific estimates from DA closely match the Census counts with the exception of three age groups. There is a large net overcount for young adults (roughly age 18–24) and a large net overcount for the population age 60–70 but there is a large net undercount for people under age 10, particularly age 0–4. Figure 3.1 also shows the effect of "age heaping" where there is a preference for reporting ages in figures ending with "0" or "5." Many of the ages ending with a "0" or a "5" are provided by proxy respondents who were often guessing at ages (West et al. 2005).

The net overcount of 18–24-year-olds is widely believed to be due to the fact that many people in this age group are counted in the home of their parents as well as where they reside most of the time…for example in a college dormitory. The net overcount of 60–70-year-olds may be due to the large portion of this population who are in the process of retiring to a new location and/or may have second homes and are counted in both places. On the other hand, there is no commonly

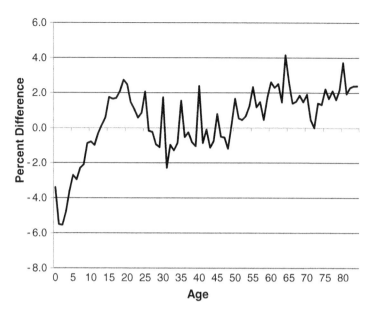

Fig. 3.1 Percent difference between 2010 census counts and DA estimates by single year of age: 0–84. *Source* May 2012 DA release

accepted explanation for the high net undercount of young children. Some potential explanations are reviewed in Chap. 7.

As Fig. 3.1 suggests, there are big differences in net undercounts and overcounts for children based on their age. Figure 3.2 shows the net undercount rates for children by single year of age and underscores the extent to which net undercount rates for children vary by age.

There are three key points that can be derived from Fig. 3.2. First, the highest net undercount rates are found among the youngest children, particularly age 0–4. More than three-quarters of the 1.3 million person net undercount for the population age 0–17 can be accounted for by those age 0–4, where the net undercount is about one million people.

Second, there is a net overcount rate for people age 14–17. Figure 3.4 shows all of the net overcount of children age 14–17 is accounted for by a high net overcount of Hispanics and Black Alone or in Combination in this age range. The DA figures released in December 2010 show an estimated net overcount of 183,000 Hispanics age 14–17, or 5.4 % difference. It is easy to imagine that at least some of this difference is due to errors in estimates of Net International Migration for this age group. The 2010 American Community Survey shows about 17 % of Hispanics age 14–17 are foreign born. DA results released May 2012 showed, Black Alone or in Combination age 14–17 was 84,000 more than the Census Count which amounts to a 2.9 % net overcount.

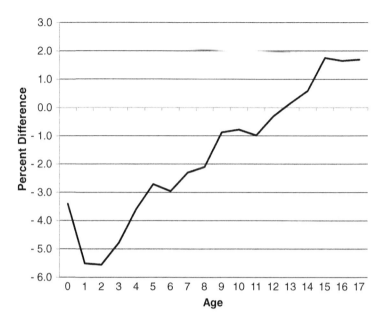

Fig. 3.2 Percent difference between 2010 census counts and DA estimates by single year of age: 0–17. *Source* May 2012 DA release

Third, there is a very clear age gradient along the age range from age 1 to 17. The net undercount rate declines steadily from age 1 to age 13 and there is a net overcount in the 14–17-year-old age group. The correlation coefficient between age and net undercount rate for the population age 0–17 is –0.96. Recall that undercounts are a negative number so this correlation means the higher the age the smaller the net undercount.

I am not aware of any published theories that attempt to explain the strong association between age and net undercount rates for children. If we had a better understanding of the reasons behind this age gradient, we might have a better understanding of why young children have such a high net undercount. This question deserves additional research attention.

Interestingly, the net undercount rate of those age 0 is much lower than the rate for those in the age 1 or 2 in the 2010 Census. This was not the case in the 2000 Census. Table 3.1 shows net undercount rates for children age 0–4 by single year of age in the 2000 and 2010 Census. Between 2000 and 2010, the net undercount decreased for age 0, but increased for every other single year of age from 1 to 4.

In that context it is worth noting that there were a couple of new instructions added to the 2010 Census questionnaire reminding respondents to include newborns and babies. One new instruction stated, "Count all people, including babies, who live and sleep here most of the time." The 2010 Census questionnaire also asks if there are any addition people staying in the housing unit on April 1 that were not listed, "including children, such as newborns babies or foster children."

Table 3.1 Net undercount by single year of age for 2000 and 2010 for the population age 0–4

Age	2000 % undercount	2010 % undercount
0	−5.0	−3.4
1	−4.4	−5.5
2	−4.5	−5.6
3	−3.3	−4.8
4	−1.8	−3.6

Source O'Hare (2014b)

Perhaps the instructions added to the 2010 Census questionnaire resulted in more people under age 1 being included in the Census. There may be lessons that can be drawn from this experience that might help the Census Bureau design better instructions for the 2020 Census questionnaire with respect to inclusion of young children.

3.2 Single Year of Age by Sex, Race, and Hispanic Origin

Several major demographic groups show the same age gradient seen for the total child population. Figure 3.3 shows net undercount estimates by single year of age for males and females, and indicates there are virtually no differences in net undercount rates between males and females at the youngest ages. When children

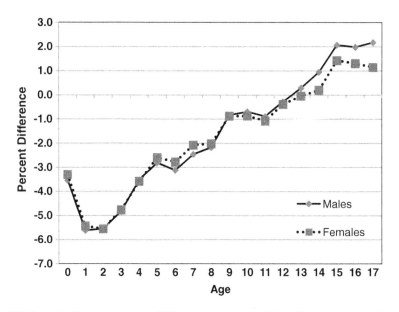

Fig. 3.3 Percent difference between 2010 census counts and DA estimates by sex and single year of age: 0–17. *Source* May 2012 DA release

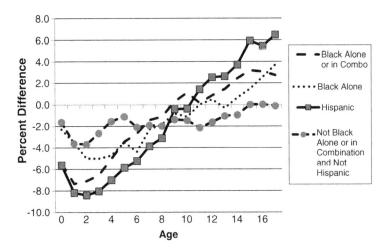

Fig. 3.4 Percent difference between 2010 census counts and DA estimates for race and Hispanic groups by single year of age: 0–17. *Source* May 2012 DA release

enter the middle teens, however, the net overcount rate of males becomes somewhat higher than that of females. I suspect the higher overcount of males in the 14–17 year age group may be related in part to undetected net immigration from abroad, where males typically outnumber females, but this deserves further research.

Figure 3.4 shows net undercount rates for children by single year of age for four population groups; (1) Black Alone, (2) Black Alone or in Combination, (3) Hispanic, and (4) a group labeled "Not Black Alone or in Combination and Not Hispanic."

The Not Black Alone or in Combination and Not Hispanic group shown in Fig. 3.4 is a derived group and not one that is used by the Census Bureau. The Not Black Alone or in Combination and Not Hispanic figures are derived by subtracting the number in the Black Alone or in Combination category and the number in the Hispanic category from the total number for each age group. This derived figure is used as a proxy population for the Non-Hispanic White population. Data from the 2010 Census shows that Non-Hispanic Whites are 90 % of the Not Black Alone or in Combination and Not Hispanic population age 0–17 and 92 % of the Not Black Alone or in Combination and Not Hispanic population age 0–4.

There is a minor problem with double counting Black Hispanics in this methodology. The 2010 Census shows that there were 285,000 children age 0–4 who were both Black Alone or in Combination and Hispanic. Since the children who are both Hispanic and Black Alone or in Combination are included in both the numerator and the denominator of the net undercount calculation for this group, the double counting should have very little impact on the net undercount rate. I believe the Not Black Alone or in Combination and Not Hispanic population provides a much better comparison group for gauging differential undercounts than the alternatives of total, Non-Black, or Non-Hispanic.

   Moreover, the usefulness of Black/Non-Black comparisons are fading, as Hispanics become a much larger share of the Non-Black population, particularly among children. In 1980, Hispanics made up 9 % of the population age 0–17, but in 2010 they were 23 %. New projections from the Census Bureau indicate Hispanics are likely to be 26 % of the child population by 2020 (U.S. Census Bureau 2014). Since Hispanics have net undercount rates that rival or exceed those of Blacks the gap between Black and Non-Black undercount rates is confounded by changing demographics of the Non-Black population. There is a similar problem comparing Hispanics to the Non-Hispanic population because the Non-Hispanic population includes Blacks.

   The age gradient reflected in Fig. 3.2 for all children is seen consistently among all the race/Hispanic groups examined here. While the exact levels and age breaks differ slightly, the same pattern is seen for Black Alone, Black Alone or in Combination, Hispanic, and Not Black Alone or in Combination and Not Hispanic children. As one moves up in age, the net undercount decreases and turns into a net overcount in the early teen years, this is followed by increasing overcounts in later years of adolescence. For the Not Black Alone or in Combination and Not Hispanic population, the coverage rate does not become an overcount as it does for the other groups in the teenage years, but there is a steady decrease in the net undercount between age 1 and 17.

   The age gradient is steeper for Blacks (Alone or in Combination) and Hispanics than for others. While Blacks and Hispanics account for a disproportionately large share of the net undercount of children age 0–4, Blacks Alone or in Combination and Hispanics account for all of the net overcount for the population age 14–17.

   The information in Fig. 3.4 raises questions about why there is a steeper gradient for Blacks (Alone or in Combination) and Hispanics than there is for other groups. Why are young Black and Hispanic children undercounted at a higher rate than others, but Blacks and Hispanics age 14–17 overcounted at a higher rate than others? I did not find any research on this question.

   The net undercount rates for Black Alone and Black Alone or in Combination are similar for ages 10–17, but differ substantially for the population below age 10 and particularly for ages 0–4 (see Fig. 3.4). The net undercount rate for the Black Alone population age 0–4 is 4.4 % but it is 6.3 % for Black Alone or in Combination in this age group (see Table 3.2).

   The only difference between the Black Alone and the Black Alone or in Combination populations is the group that is Black in Combination. The 2010 DA estimate show 3,195,000 Black Alone age 0–4 and 3,905,000 Black Alone or in Combination age 0–4. By subtraction this means there were 710,000 in the Black in Combination category in the DA estimates. The 2010 Census counted 3,055,000 Black Alone age 0–4 and 3,658,000 Black Alone and in Combination age 0–4. By subtraction there were 603,000 Black in Combination in the Census counts. For the population age 0–4, the net undercount rate for Blacks in Combination is about 15 %.

   The relatively high net undercount rate for young Blacks Alone or in Combination and the difference between the net undercount rate for young Black Alone (4.4 %) and young Black Alone or in Combination (6.3 %) raises

Table 3.2 Difference between 2010 census counts and middle series DA estimates for the population age 0–4, by sex, race and Hispanic origin

	2010 census count (in 1000 s)	2010 DA estimate (in 1000 s)	Numeric difference between census count and DA estimate	Percent difference between census count and DA estimate
Total	20,201	21,171	−970	−4.6
Female	9,882	10,353	−471	−4.5
Male	10,320	10,821	−501	−4.6
Black alone	3,055	3,195	−140	−4.4
Black alone or in combination	3,658	3,905	−247	−6.3
Not black alone	17,146	17,976	−830	−4.6
Not black alone or in combination	16,544	17,268	−724	−4.2
Hispanic	5,114	5,528	−414	−7.5
Not Hispanic	15,087	15,643	−556	−3.6
Not black alone and not Hispanic	12,032	12,448	−416	−3.3
Not black alone or in combination and not Hispanic	11,429	11,738	−309	−2.7

Notes The "not black alone or in combination and not Hispanic" Category and the "not black alone and not Hispanic category" are not categories used by the Census Bureau. Please see the text for an explanation of how the figures for these categories were derived. DA estimates by Hispanic origin are only available for the December 2010 DA release
Sources U.S. Census Bureau (2010, 2012)

several questions about how accurately data from birth certificates can be coded to match self-reported (or parent reported) data from the Census. This issue was discussed in Chap. 2. Recall that new birth certificates were introduced in 2003, which allowed parents to mark more than one race for the first time, and the number of states using the new birth certificate form increased over time. The switch to the more than one race option for parents on the birth certificates starting in 2003 corresponds to the increase in the number of newborns classified as Black in Combination which is most heavily reflected in the population 0–4 in 2010.

3.3 The Population Age 0–4

Since children age 0–4 have the highest net undercount rate of any age group in the 2010 Decennial Census, the remainder of this Chapter will focus on that age group. It should be noted that young children not only have the highest net undercount rate of any age group, the magnitude of the difference between the

DA estimate and the Census count for age 0–4 is larger than any other age group regardless of the direction of the difference (see Fig. 3.1).

Table 3.2 shows the 2010 Census net undercount rates and population numbers for age 0–4 by various demographic characteristics. All groups had a relatively high net undercount rate, but there are substantial differences among groups.

The net undercount rate for males and females was nearly identical at 4.6 and 4.5 %, respectively. This contrasts with adults, particularly young adults, where there are substantial differences in Census coverage rates by sex. Given the similarity of living arrangements for young children, it is not surprising that there is little difference in net undercount rates by sex for young children.

The net undercount rate for all people age 0–4 was 4.6 % but there were notable differences by race and Hispanic Origin. The net undercount rate for Black Alone or in Combination age 0–4 was 6.3 %, the rate for Black Alone was 4.4 %, and the net undercount rate for Hispanic children in this age range was 7.5 %. For the Not Black Alone or in Combination and Not Hispanic category, which is a proxy group for Non-Hispanic White population, the net undercount rate for age 0–4 was 2.7 %.

The high net undercount rate of young Black and Hispanic children relative to others is consistent with much of the past research on Census undercount differentials which shows racial minorities often have higher net undercount rates than others (Fein 1989; Anderson et al. 2012; West et al. 2014).

The fact that Hispanic children have a higher net undercount rate than other groups in the 0–4 age range is consistent with new research (Van Hook et al. 2014, p. 699) which concludes that "The U.S. Census and ACS data miss substantial numbers of children of Mexican immigrants…" The fact that young Hispanics have a higher net undercount rate than any other group is also consistent with the extent to which this group has many of the Hard-to-Count characteristics identified by the Census Bureau (Bruce and Robinson 2003; Erdman and Bates 2014) such as being highly mobile, disproportionately in rental housing, and more likely to experience language barriers.

The only DA data available for Hispanics is from the December 2010 release, but this estimate of the undercount for Hispanics age 0–4, may have a slight upward bias. Because it takes the National Center for Health Statistics a few years to process data from the birth and death certificates to produce final reports, the 2010 DA release had to rely on estimates of births and deaths for 2008, 2009 and the first quarter of 2010, rather than observed data.

The revised DA estimates for the total and the Black groups that were released in May 2012, benefited from the availability of actual birth and death records for 2008, 2009 and the first quarter of 2010, and the observed vital event data indicate the Census Bureau's estimates for the number of births in 2008–2010 period used in the 2010 DA release were a little too high and thus the DA Population Estimates for the youngest ages were a little high. Since there were no updated DA estimates for Hispanics in the May 2012 DA release, I had to rely on the Middle Series from the December 2010 release which are based on estimated vital events for 2008, 2009, and the first quarter of 2010. However, this is likely to have only a very small impact. For the overall population the addition of actual birth and death data changed the net undercount rate for age 0–4 from 4.7 % in the December 2010 DA release to 4.6 % in the May 2012 DA release.

The combined groups of young Black Alone or in Combination and young Hispanic children account for about two-thirds of the total net undercount for age 0–4 even though they only account for about 40 % of the population in this age range. Moreover, the net undercount of Black Alone or in Combination and Hispanic children age 0–4 (about 661,000), accounts for more than half of the total net undercount of all people under age 18 (1.3 million) even though this group comprises only 11 % of that population age 0–17. This suggests that households with young Black or Hispanic children should be a target in efforts to reduce the net undercount of young children in the 2020 Census.

3.4 Summary

In the 2010 U.S. Decennial Census, the small overcount for the total population (+0.1 %) masks notable differences between children and adults. The net undercount rate for all children age 0–17 was 1.7 % while adults had a net overcount rate of 0.7 %.

The net undercount rate for all children conceals large differences for children in different age groups. Age 0–4 had the highest net undercount rate (4.6 %) of any age group in the 2010 Census. The net undercount for age 0–4 in the 2010 Census was almost one million people. The net undercount rate for age 0–4 was more than twice as high as the next closest age group (age 5–9). In contrast to the relatively high net undercount rate for young children, the population age 14–17 had a net overcount (1.4 %).

It is clear that people under age 18 should not be treated as a homogeneous age group with respect to Census coverage as has sometimes been done in the past. Analyses that fail to make a distinction among age groups of children are likely to find interpretation of findings difficult. The explanation for why young children experience a high net undercount is likely to be quite different than the explanation for why the population age 14–17 have a net overcount. Moreover, combining the age 0–4 population and the age 14–17 population into one group, masks the differences between the Census and the DA estimates in both groups.

In addition, there is a clear and strong age gradient from age 1 to 17. Increased age is correlated with lower net undercounts for the population age 1–17. There are no theories I am aware of to explain the strong linear relationship between Census coverage rates and age among children.

Consistent with much of the Census undercount literature, the net undercount rates for Blacks Alone or in Combination and Hispanics were above average. The net undercount for Hispanics age 0–4 (7.5 %) and for Black Alone or in Combination age 0–4 (6.3 %) were more than twice as high as the rate for the Not Black Alone or in Combination not Hispanic (a proxy for Non-Hispanic Whites) which experienced an estimated net undercount of 2.7 %.

The increasing complexity of trying to measure race and issues with trying to align racial data from birth certificates and the Census suggest coverage estimates for the Black child population should be used cautiously. The experience of young children in the 2010 Census suggests the difficulties trying to match racial categories from births certificates to the Census is likely to be a bigger problem in the future.

References

Anderson, M. J., Citro, C. F., & Salvo, J. J. (Eds.), (2012). *Encyclopedia of the U.S. census: From the constitution to the American Community Survey (ACS)*. Beverley Hills: Sage Publications.

Bruce, A., & Robinson, J. G. (2003) The planning database: Its development and use as an effective tool in census 2000. In *Paper presented at the Annual Meeting of the Southern Demographic Association*. Arlington, VA.

Erdman, C., & Bates, N. (2014). *The census bureau mail return rate challenge: Crowdsourcing to development hard-to-count scores*. Washington, DC: U.S. Census Bureau.

Fein, D. J. (1989). *The social sources of census omission: Racial and ethnic differences in omission rates in recent U.S. censuses*. Dissertation, Department of Sociology, Princeton University, Princeton NJ.

O'Hare, W. P. (2014a). Assessing net coverage error for young children in the 2010 U.S. decennial census. In *Center for survey measurement study series (survey methodology #2014–02)*. Washington, DC: U.S. Census Bureau.

O'Hare, W. P. (2014b). Historical examination of net coverage error for children in the U.S. decennial census: 1950 to 2010. In *Center for survey measurement study series (survey methodology #2014–03)*. Washington, DC: U.S. Census Bureau.

U.S. Census Bureau. (2010). Tables released at December 2010 Conference.

U.S. Census Bureau. (2012). Documentation for the revised 2010 demographic analysis middle series estimates.

U.S. Bureau of the Census. (2014). U.S. population projections: 2014–2060: Release number CB14-TPS.86. Washington, DC: U.S. Census Bureau.

Van Hook, J., Bean, F. D., Bachmeier, J. D., & Tucker, C. (2014). Recent trends in coverage of mexican-born population of the United States, results from applying multiple methods across time. In *Demography*, published on line Feb 26, 2014. doi:10.1007/s13524-014-0280-2.

Velkoff, V. (2011). Demographic evaluation of the 2010 census. In *Paper presented at the 2011 PAA Annual Conference*. Washington, DC.

West, K. K., Robinson, J. G., & Bentley, M. (2005). Did proxy respondents cause age heaping in the census 2000? In *Paper delivered at the Joint Statistical Meetings: ASA Section on Survey Research Methods*.

West, K., Devine, J., & Robinson, J. G. (2014). An assessment of historical demographic analysis estimates for the black male birth cohorts of 1935–39. In *Paper presented at the Annual Meeting of the American Statistical Association*. Boston, MA.

Chapter 4
Historical Examination of Net Coverage for Children in the U.S. Decennial Census: 1950 to 2010

Abstract U.S. Decennial Censuses from 1950 to 2010 are examined to distill patterns in net undercount rates by age. The coverage rates of children are compared to those of adults then patterns for young children are compared to older children. From 1950 to 1980, the net undercount rates of all age groups fell and the differences among the undercount rates for different age groups were not large. The net undercount rate of young children went from 1.4 % in 1980 to 4.6 % in the 2010 Census. Over the same time period, the net undercount rate of adults continued the decline witnessed between 1950 and 1980. The net undercount rates for Blacks are higher than those of Non-Blacks in every census from 1950 to 2010.

Keywords Net coverage · Undercount · Children

The net undercount rate for children of all ages and the high net undercount rate for young children in the 2010 Census raises questions about the net undercount of children in the Censuses historically. How do the net undercount rates for children in the 2010 U.S. Census compare to U.S. Census results in the past? Have children had a higher net undercount rate than adults in the past? Have younger children had a higher net undercount rate than older children in the past?

Despite data showing a high net undercount rate for children more than fifty years ago, I have been unable to find any reports or systematic examination of the trends over time in the net undercount of children in the U.S. Censuses. Looking at the trends from 1950 to 1980 it is understandable that the net undercount rates of young children were not singled out for attention because the net undercount of young children was not much different than the undercount for the total population, as shown later in this chapter. However, since 1980 it has been clear that the net undercount rates for young children have been very different than those of adults.

This chapter provides a detailed and systematic examination of the net undercount of children (the population age 0–17) in general and young children (population age 0–4) in particular in every U.S. Census since 1950. Differences between Black and Non-Black child populations are also examined to the extent possible given the changing racial categories used in the Decennial Censuses.

4.1 Data Sources

The time series examined here starts with the 1950 Census. DA estimates for the 1950 through 2000 Censuses are taken from a Census Bureau Working Paper (O'Hare 2014). The data in the working paper are derived from a Census Bureau internal file, which provides DA estimates of the population by age, sex, and race (Black and Non-Black) for each U.S. Census year. The corresponding counts from the U.S. Decennial Censuses are also available on this internal file. The specific sources for the 2010 Census data are given in Chap. 3.

These DA estimates are based on an on-going compilation of birth and death certificate data and Net International Migration estimates. Because the internal Census Bureau historical series has been updated regularly, the figures presented here may differ in very minor ways from data published previously by the Census Bureau.

Data in this chapter are presented in two formats. Tables 4.1, 4.2, and 4.3 provide the data in tabular form but many of the key trends are better illustrated with graphs so key data from the tables are also presented in graphic form. The graphics provide a clearer picture of trends while the tables provide detailed statistical data that some readers may prefer.

Table 4.1 Net undercount for age groups 1950–2010

	1950	1960	1970	1980	1990	2000	2010
All races all ages	−3.7	−2.5	−2.4	−0.9	−1.6	−0.1	0.1
All races age 0–4	−4.7	−2.4	−3.6	−1.4	−3.7	−3.8	−4.6
All races age 5–13	−2.3	−2.4	−2.5	−0.7	−1.6	−0.2	−1.4
All races age 14–17	−2.3	−1.5	0.2	0.4	−0.4	1.5	
All races age 0–17	−3.5	−2.3	−2.5	−0.7	−1.8	−0.7	−1.7
All races Age 18+	−3.8	−2.6	−2.3	−1	−1.6	0.1	0.7
Gap between adults and young children (adults–young children)	0.9	−0.2	1.3	0.5	2.1	3.9	5.3
Gap between adults and all children (adults–all children)	−0.3	−0.3	0.2	−0.3	0.2	0.7	2.4

Source O'Hare (2014)

Table 4.2 Net undercount for children by single year of age: 1950–2010

Age	1950	1960	1970	1980	1990	2000	1950–2000 mean	2010
Ages 0–17	−3.7	−2.5	−2.4	−0.9	−1.6	−0.1	−1.9	
0	−11.2	−2.3	−3.0	0.8	−3.0	−5.0	−3.9	−3.4
1	−7.2	−1.9	−3.5	−2.7	−4.2	−4.4	−4.0	−5.5
2	−2.6	−2.9	−4.7	−2.9	−4.3	−4.5	−3.6	−5.6
3	−0.9	−3.0	−4.0	−1.6	−4.3	−3.3	−2.9	−4.8
4	−0.6	−2.0	−2.8	−0.8	−2.9	−1.8	−1.8	−3.6
5	−2.4	−1.5	−3.1	−1.1	−2.8	−1.5	−2.1	−2.7
6	−3.3	−2.4	−2.8	−1.3	−2.9	−2.0	−2.4	−3.0
7	−3.0	−1.4	−2.7	0.2	−2.7	−1.2	−1.8	−2.3
8	−1.1	−3.4	−4.1	−3.2	−6.3	−1.5	−3.3	−2.1
9	−3.2	−3.1	−3.2	−0.6	0.4	−0.6	−1.7	−0.9
10	−1.0	−2.5	0.8	1.0	0.8	1.0	0.0	−0.8
11	−5.4	−2.1	−2.8	−0.3	−0.4	0.9	−1.7	−1.0
12	−0.4	−1.7	−2.3	−0.8	−0.6	1.5	−0.7	−0.3
13	−0.8	−3.4	−2.4	−0.3	0.1	1.5	−0.9	0.1
14	−4.3	0.3	−0.8	0.0	0.3	2.1	−0.4	0.6
15	−4.1	−2.3	−1.1	0.6	0.5	2.8	−0.6	1.8
16	−3.0	−3.5	−2.1	0.3	0.4	2.5	−0.9	1.6
17	−5.6	−2.7	−1.9	−0.2	1.8	1.8	−1.1	1.7

Source O'Hare (2014)

Table 4.3 Summary of net undercount rates of black and non-black children age 0–4 and 0–17: 1950–2010

	Black age 0–4	Black age 0–17	Non-black age 0–4	Non-black age 0–17
1950	−8.4	−6.0	−4.2	−3.2
1960	−6.0	−4.7	−1.8	−2.0
1970	−9.5	−5.9	−2.5	−2.0
1980	−7.8	−3.6	−0.2	−0.1
1990	−7.6	−5.3	−3.0	−1.1
2000	−5.4	−1.3	−3.5	−0.5
	Black alone 0–4	Black alone age 0–17	Not black alone 0–4	Not black alone age 0–17
2010	−4.4	−0.6	−4.6	−4.2
	Black alone or in combination age 0–4	Black alone or in combination age 0–17	Not black alone or in combination age 0–4	Not black alone or in combination age 0–17
2010	−6.3	−1.5	−1.9	−1.7

Source O'Hare (2014)

4.2 Historic Patterns in the Net Undercount of Adults and Children

Examination of net Census coverage rates from 1950 to 2010 indicates a significant and steady reduction in the net undercount for the total population. Figure 4.1 shows that the net undercount rate for the total population has fallen nearly every decade since 1950, reaching a small net overcount in 2010.

However, when the overall trend shown in Fig. 4.1 is decomposed by age, a somewhat different story emerges. Figure 4.2 shows net undercount rates for the adult population (age 18 and older) and the child population (age 0–17) for each U.S. Census from 1950 to 2010. Figure 4.2 shows that there have been two very distinct periods between 1950 and 2010 in terms of the net undercount trends of adults and children. Between 1950 and 1980, the net undercount rates for both groups declined steadily and the differences between the net undercount rate of

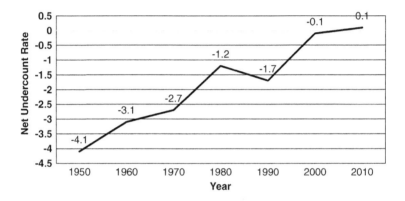

Fig. 4.1 Net undercount rates for the total population: 1950–2010. *Source* O'Hare (2014)

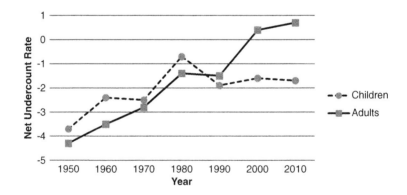

Fig. 4.2 Net undercount rates for children and adults: 1950–2010. *Source* O'Hare (2014)

children and adults were not large. Specifically, the net undercount rate of the adult population went from 3.8 % in 1950 to 1.4 % in 1980 while the net undercount rate for children fell from 3.5 to 0.7 % over the same period. Note these figure are for all children not young children.

Following the 1980 Census, the net undercount rates of children and adults began to diverge. The coverage rates for adults continued the improvement seen in the 1950–1980 period while the net undercount rates for children increased following 1980. Specifically, the coverage rates for adults went from 1.4 % net undercount rate in 1980 to a 0.7 % net overcount rate in 2010. The net undercount rate for children went from 0.7 % in 1980 to 1.7 % in 2010.

4.3 Net Undercount of Children by Age

The overall trend in the net undercount rates of children from 1950 to 2010 reflects very different trajectories for children in different age groups. Figure 4.3 shows the trends in net Census undercount rates since 1950 for three age groups of children; age 0–4, age 5–13, and age 14–17. These age groupings were used because these groups have very different net Census coverage rates in the 2010 U.S. Decennial Census. In addition, these age groups have some social significance because they roughly correspond to the preschool-age population, the elementary and middle school-age population, and the high school-age population.

Figure 4.3 shows that there has been growing divergence in Census coverage rates for children of different ages and that the differences among age groups are more striking after 1980 than before.

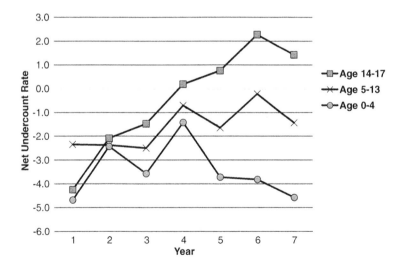

Fig. 4.3 Net undercount rates for different age groups of children: 1950–2010. *Source* O'Hare (2014)

Perhaps the most striking aspect of Fig. 4.3 is the change in the net undercount rates of young children following the 1980 Census. Between 1980 and 2010, the net undercount rate for young children increased from 1.4 to 4.6 %. Recall that over the same period the net undercount rate of adults continued the improvement that had been witnessed during the 1950–1980 period. What happened after 1980 that altered the trajectory of net undercount rates for young children? The profession has not offered any answers to this question.

Interestingly, the net undercount rates for Canada showed a similar trend (see Table 6.1). The net undercount rate for the population age 0–4 was 1.2 % in the 1981 Canadian Census, but it was 3.4 % in 2011 Census. The trend over time in Canada has not been quite as linear as the one in the U.S. but there has generally been an upward trend in the net undercount of young children in Canada since 1981.

Similar to the adult population, the net undercount rates for the population age 14–17 has shown a steady decline since 1980, reaching a net overcount of 1.4 % in 2010.

Relative to young children and the population age 14–17, children in middle childhood (age 5–13) experienced fairly stable net undercount rates between 1950 and 2010. The net undercount rates for this age group varied from a low net undercount of 0.7 % in 1980, to a high of 2.5 % in 1970. Even though the net undercount rate for those age 5–13 has been relatively small, it is worth noting that there has been a net undercount for the population age 5–13 in every Census since 1950.

The net undercount rate for young children in 2010 (4.6 %) is almost the same as the rate experienced by this age group in the 1950 Census (4.7 %). Over the same time period the net undercount rate for the population age 14–17 fell from 5.2 % to a net overcount of 1.5 %; a 6.7 percentage point swing. This underscores the importance of examining children by age not only in terms of current results but in historic trends as well.

Another perspective on the data in Fig. 4.3 is expressed by Hogan (2013). If one ignores the results from the 1980 Census, there has been relatively little movement in the net undercount of young children between 1950 and 2010. If one discounts the 1980 results, the net undercount of young children was between −2.4 and −4.6 % in every Census from 1950 to 2010 without much of a temporal pattern before or after 1980. The results for 1980 may be different from the other Censuses because there was a major effort to reduce the undercount in 1980, in part, because of political pressure for an adjustment of Census figures in the face of persistent undercount differentials.

From this perspective the question is not what happened after 1980, but rather why has there been consistently high net undercount rates for young children since 1950 while the net undercount rate for adults steadily improved? The profession has not offered any answers to this question.

Figure 4.4 shows the gap between the Census coverage rates of adults and young children from 1950 to 2010 in a more direct way. Between 1950 and 1980 the gap was relatively small and stable, varying between 0 and 1.1 percentage points. Figure 4.4 shows the divergence after 1980 is striking and has been increasing steadily reaching 5.3 % age points in 2010.

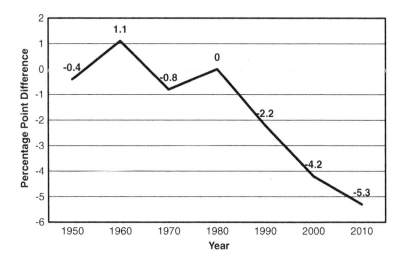

Fig. 4.4 Gap in net undercount rates of adults (age 18+) and young children (age 0–4): 1950–2010. *Source* O'Hare (2014)

4.4 Historic Patterns by Single Year of Age

The 2010 results show a clear age gradient in terms of net undercounts and net overcounts for children (see Fig. 3.2). Increased age is correlated with lower net undercounts. In 2010, the correlation between net undercount rates and age for children was—0.96. Has there been a similar gradient by age in terms of the net undercounts and overcounts of children in the past Censuses?

Graphing the net undercount rates by single year of age for every Census since 1950 produced a graph that made it difficult to identify trends because of the high number of data points. As an alternative, Fig. 4.5 shows the net undercount rate of children by single year of age for the 2010 U.S. Census compared with the average net undercount rates over every U.S. Census from 1950 to 1970 and a second average from 1980 to 2000 by single year of age from 0 to 17.

Age heaping on age 10 is evident in Fig. 4.5, particularly in the 1950–1970 period. If the age heaping could be corrected, it is likely that the relationship between age and net undercount rates in the past would be smoother.

The age gradient in the Census is becoming steeper. In the data from 1950 to 1970, there is almost no trend with respect to net undercounts by age. In the data from 1980 to 2000, there is a gradient, but it is not as steep as that seen in the 2010 data.

Table 4.4 shows the same data in a different way. Table 4.4 shows correlations between age and Census coverage rates for children for all of the Census years since 1950.

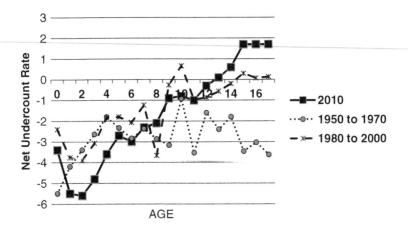

Fig. 4.5 Net undercount rates by single year of age: 2010 and mean of 1950–1970 and 1980–2000

Table 4.4 Correlations between age and net undercount rates by single-year of age for the population age 0–17: 1950–2010

1950	1960	1970	1980	1990	2000	2010
−0.19	0.27	0.76	0.76	0.69	0.82	0.96

Source O'Hare (2014)

In 1950 there was a negative correlation between age and net coverage rates for children and a low positive correlation in 1960. Since 1970, the correlation has been relatively high and positive (i.e. increasing age associated with lower net undercount rates) with the 2010 correlation being the highest observed here.

4.5 Trends by Race from 1950 to 2000

Some of the issues regarding the difficulty of using the DA method to measure net undercounts by race were discussed in Chap. 2. The undercount data for Blacks in the 2010 Census is substantially different than for earlier Censuses because of the new Black Alone and Black Alone or in Combination categories used in 2010 DA. Prior to 2010, the Census Bureau produced a DA figure for Black, but not for Black Alone or Black Alone or in Combination. I look first at the trends from 1950 to 2000 where Black and Non-Black categories have been relatively consistent over time.

Different data series have been used to compare Census and DA results for the Black population over time. Prior to the 1980 Census, the U.S. Census figures that were used to compare with the DA estimates for Blacks were the reported U.S. Census figures for Blacks. In 1980, the Census Bureau compared the DA estimates to a modified file which assigned people in the Some Other Race category to a Black or Non-Black category (Fay et al. 1988). In 1990, the Census Bureau used the race

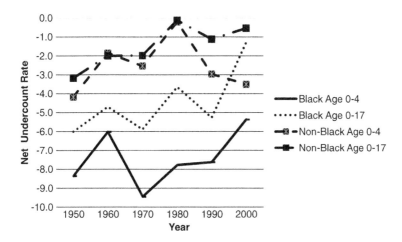

Fig. 4.6 Net undercount rates for black and non-black populations age 0–4 and 0–17: 1950–2000

of father from the birth certificate to assign race to newborns and then compared DA estimates for Blacks to the MARS (Modified Age, Race, and Sex) file from the Census (Robinson et al. 1993). For 2000, the Census Bureau used race of father from the birth certificate to assign race to newborns and then DA estimates were compared to an average of Black Alone and Black Alone or in Combination based on the Census Bureau's modified race file (U.S. Bureau of the Census 2003).

Figure 4.6 shows the net undercount rate of Black children and Non-Black children for each U.S. Census from 1950 to 2000 for age 0–17 and age 0–4, based on data described above. In every U.S. Census from 1950 to 2000, the net undercount rate for Black children was higher than that for Non-Black children in both age groups. However, the gap has narrowed. For young children it has narrowed because the net undercount rate for the Black population has decreased and the Non-Black rate increased (mostly reflected in changes from 1980 to 2000). The net undercount rate for young Black children in 1950 was 6.0 % but it had fallen to 1.3 % in 2000. The net undercount rate for young Non-Black children fell from 3.2 % 1950 to 0.1 % in 1980, but then increased to 3.5 % in 2000. Recall Hispanic have become a much larger share of the Non-Black population over this period.

For children age 0–17 the narrowing is largely due to decreases in the net undercount rate for the Black population. There has been little change in the net undercount rate of the Non-Black population age 0–17 since 1980.

4.6   Trends by Race from 2000 to 2010

The bottom panel in Table 4.2 shows the 2010 net undercount rate for all children and young children in four race categories: (1) Black Alone, (2) Black Alone or in Combination, (3) Not Black Alone, and (4) Not Black Alone or in Combination.

The net undercount rate reported by the Census Bureau for Blacks age 0–4 in the 2000 Census was 5.4 %. Recall that the reported net undercount rate for Blacks in 2000 was the DA estimate compared to an average of the Black Alone and Black Alone or in Combination Census figures.

Distilling change in the net undercount rate for Black children between 2000 and 2010 is challenging. If one compares the net undercount rate of Black Alone in 2010 (4.4 %) to the Black rate for 2000 (5.4 %) it suggests that the net undercount rate for the Black population fell between 2000 and 2010. But if one compares the net undercount rate for Black Alone or in Combination in 2010 (6.3 %) to the Black undercount rate in 2000 it suggests that the net undercount rate for Blacks increased between 2000 and 2010. It may be worth noting here that the Black Alone or in Combination population better reflects the spirit of U.S. Office of Management and Budget (2001) regulation regarding use of data based on more than one race category. It is also worth pointing out that both the Black Alone and the Black Alone or in Combination net undercount rate for 2010 are higher than the rate for the Non-Hispanic White proxy population shown in Chap. 3.

The complications of trying to assess trends over time with the new multi-race concept reflects a larger issue about how people are categorized by race in the U.S. federal statistical system (Prewitt 2013). In the 1970s and 1990s the federal government revised the way it categorized people by race and Hispanic Origin status in the federal statistical system. Perhaps the issue will be revisited by again before long.

4.7   Hispanics 2000 to 2010

The historical data on the net undercount of Hispanic children is very limited but examination of data from 2000 and 2010 show the net undercount rate for young Hispanics has been relatively stable. The net undercount rate for Hispanic children age 0–4 in 2000 was 7.7 % compared to 7.5 % in 2010.

4.8   Summary

Analysis presented here shows that the net undercount rates for all age groups fell from 1950 to 1980, but after 1980 there was growing divergence of Census coverage rates for young children and adults. The net undercount rate for adults continued the downward trend seen since 1950 and there were actually overcounts in 2000 and 2010. For young children, however, net undercount rate went from 1.4 % in 1980 to 4.6 % in 2010.

The data presented here also underscore how different age groups of children have very different Census coverage trends over time. The Census coverage rates of young children and 14-to-17-year-olds have been diverging since 1980. Young children have increasing net undercount rates and the population age 14–17 have decreasing net undercount rates.

The age gradient reflecting the association between age and net undercount rates has increased over time. In the 2010 U.S. Census there was nearly a perfect correlation between and age and net undercount rates for the population age 0–17. In the 1950 Census there was almost no statistical relationship between age and net undercount rates for children.

Data show that the net undercount rate for Black children age 0–4 and age 0–17 were higher than those for Non-Black children consistently from 1950 to 2000. However the gap between undercount rates for Black and Non-Black children narrowed in recent years, in part due to lower net undercount rates for Black children and in part to higher net undercount rates for Non-Black children. The increased net undercount rates for Non-Black children may be due to the fact that a growing share of Non-Black children are Hispanic.

In 2010, for the first time, estimates were provided for Black Alone and Black Alone or in Combination. Analysis provided here underscores the difficulty of assessing Census coverage for Blacks and Non-Blacks over time, in part due to changes in the racial categories used and in part because Hispanics have become a larger share of the Non-Black population. The complexity of trying to match racial categories in the birth and death certificate data with data reported in the Census questionnaire highlights the many challenges the Census Bureau faces in producing undercount and overcount rates by race using the DA method. Moreover, the production of these two more nuanced race categories (Black Alone/Black Alone or in Combination) complicates comparisons with earlier data by race. These results underscore the importance of the Census Bureau's research on measuring race.

References

Fay, R. E., Passel, J. S., Robinson, J. G., & Cowan, C. D. (1988). *The coverage of the population in the 1980 census,* U.S. Census of Population and Housing, Evaluation and Research Reports, PHC80-E4, U.S Census Bureau, Washington DC.

Hogan, H. (2013). Presentation at the 2013 joint statistical meetings, Montreal.

O'Hare, W. P. (2014). Historical examination of net coverage error for children in the U.S. decennial census: 1950 to 2010. In *Center for Survey Measurement Study Series (Survey Methodology #2014-03).* U.S. Census Bureau, Washington DC.

Prewitt, K. (2013). *What is Your Race?: The Census and our flawed efforts to classify americans.* Princeton University Press, Princeton, NJ.

Robinson, J. G., Bashir, A., Das Dupta, P., & Woodward, K. A. (1993). Estimates of population coverage in the 1990 United States U.S. decennial census based on demographic analysis. *Journal of the American Statistical Association, 88*(423), 1061–1071.

U.S. Census Bureau. (2003). *Technical Assessment of A.C.E. Revision II,* U.S. Census Bureau, Washington DC.

U.S. Office of Management and Budget. (2001). Guidance on aggregation and allocation of data on race for use in civil rights monitoring and enforcement.

Chapter 5
State and County Level 2010 U.S. Census Coverage Rates for Young Children

Abstract The national net undercount rate for young children masks large differences across states and counties. State-level census coverage rates for age 0–4
range from a net undercount of 10.2 % in Arizona to a 2.1 % overcount in North
Dakota. State net undercount rates for children age 0–4 are correlated with state
population size, racial/Hispanic composition as well as several Hard-to-Count
characteristics such as linguistic isolation, education, and employment. The net
undercount of young children is concentrated in the largest counties. The 128 largest counties, all with populations of 500,000 or more, account of 77 % of the total
net undercount for age 0–4.

Keywords Subnational census coverage · State undercount rates · County
undercount rates

To date there has been little information on how the national Census undercount is distributed among sub-national geographic units such as states and counties. This Chapter
addresses the net undercount of young children at the state and county level and also
examines correlates of variation in net undercount rates across units of geography.

One of the major limitations of the Demographic Analysis (DA) technique for
measuring the Census undercounts for most demographic groups is that it can
only be applied at the national level. However, young children are an exception to
this rule. For the population under age 10, the U.S. Census Bureau's post-Census
Population Estimates provide a population estimate that is independent of the Census.
This approach cannot be used for the population over age 10 because the 2010
Estimates are derived from the 2000 Census, so the estimates are not independent
of the census.

Specifically, the Census Bureau's Vintage 2010 State and County Population
Estimates for young children provide an opportunity to assess sub-national Census
results. The Vintage 2010 State and County Population Estimates for those under

---

This Chapter draws heavily on an article by O'Hare (2014c).

age 10 are based on births, deaths, and net migration, which is essentially the same demographic accounting equation used in DA.

In this Chapter state and county-level net undercounts of young children are developed by comparing the U.S. Census Bureau's Vintage 2010 Population Estimates for the population age 0–4 to the 2010 U.S. Census counts for this age group. The analysis focuses on the population age 0–4, rather than 0–9, because the 2010 DA analysis shows the net undercount for the 0–4 age group is much higher than that for the age group 5–9 (see Chap. 3). The 2010 national undercount rate for the population age 0–4 based on DA is 4.6 % compared to only 2.2 % for age 5–9. Therefore it is important to examine the population age 0–4 separately from those aged 5–9. At the same time, it is worth noting there is a very high positive correlation across states in the net undercount rates of the population 0–4 and the population age 5–9 ($r = +0.97$). Consequently, patterns observed for the population age 0–4, are also likely to be seen in the population age 5–9.

The case for developing sub-national estimates of Census coverage was made eloquently more than 30 years ago by Siegel et al. (1977, p. 1),

> The importance of Census counts of the population in determining political representation, in the disbursement of public funds, and in the planning, conduct, and evaluation of various private and public program has aroused considerable interest in the accuracy of Census counts for States and smaller political units and, particularly, in the availability of estimates of coverage for these areas in the last Census.

States are a useful geographic unit to use for this analysis because most of the past work on sub-national Census coverage has focused on states. In addition, the Population Estimates at the state level are more accurate than those for counties or other smaller geographic units so the undercount estimates for states are more robust than those for counties. Yowell and Devine (2013, Table 2) found the mean absolute percentage error for county Population Estimates was three times that of states in assessing the 2010 Population Estimates. This is consistent with the general principal that population estimates for larger places (in population size) are typically more accurate than smaller places (Felton 1986; Davis 1994; O'Hare 1988).

States are also a useful unit of analysis for geo-political reasons. In terms of public policies related to children, states are much more important than counties and their importance has been growing. According to Gormely (2012, p. 100),

> The role of state government in funding and regulating elementary and secondary education has long been of critical importance, and state expenditures on child health through Medicaid and Child Health Insurance Program (SCHIP), have increased significantly in recent years. More than federal government, state governments devote a substantial percentage of their time and their financial resources to children.

5.1 Background

Past research on sub-national assessments of the U.S. Census results are limited. Much of the public and political interest in sub-national undercounts was first generated by Hill and Steffes (1973) who used a synthetic estimation technique to produce state and local area undercount estimates of the 1970 Census results.

Following the 1970 Decennial Census, Siegel et al. (1977) also examined Census coverage for states and for various population groups defined by race and age. Several different approaches were used with mixed results.

Following the 1980 Census Isaki and colleagues (Isaki et al. 1985) examined a couple of ideas for developing estimates of net undercounts at subnational levels. These efforts involved use of both the PES and the DA results.

Following the 1990 Decennial Census, Robinson et al. (1993) offered a set of 1990 Census undercount estimates for states for the total population (all ages). There were no estimates for children and the estimates were only evaluated at the multi-state regional level. The authors also proposed alternatives for evaluating the 2000 Census at the state and sub-state levels and listed several reasons why such an evaluation is needed. Robinson and Kobilarkic (1995) also discuss sub-national evaluations the 1990 Census using a DA-like approach.

Adlakha et al. (2003) used Census Bureau Post Census Population Estimates to assess the state-level 2000 U.S. Census counts for the population age 0–9, but their analysis did not go below the multi-state regional level and did not show data for the population age 0–4 separately.

Based on unpublished Census Bureau data, Darga (1999, p. 32) examined sub-national undercounts of children under age 10 in the 1990 Census. However, his estimates are based on the 1990 Post Enumeration Survey rather than DA and they were only examined for multi-state regions, not states.

Cohn (2011) compared the Census Bureau's state Population Estimates to the 2010 Census counts for the total population (i.e. all ages) but did not break out young children separately. Cohn concludes that the Census counts and the Population Estimates are quite close for most states in terms of total population.

Mayol-Garcia and Robinson (2011) examined differences between Population Estimates and Census counts for states for age 0–4 and age 0–9 populations in the 2010 Census but only provided limited results and did not explore any patterns across states. However, regarding the state-level data on the net undercounts of the population age 0–4, Mayol-Garcia and Robinson (2011, p. 3) note, "The relatively large differences noted nationally for 0–4 year olds are observed at the state level as well." O'Hare (2013, 2014a, b) also provides some preliminary analysis of 2010 net Census coverage rates for young children at the sub-national level.

Based on their analysis of 2000 U.S. Census data, Adlakha et al. (2003, p. v) recommended we, "expand the current demographic analysis to include sub-national benchmarks in the 2010 Census evaluation." Mayol-Garcia and Robinson (2011) also conclude, "More studies are needed on the patterns of this population age group compared to the results of the previous Censuses." The present analysis responds to those recommendations.

The present analysis extends previous research by examining state and county level Census coverage for young children in more detail and examining factors correlated with variations in state differences in net Census coverage rates for young children. First, the state net undercount rates for age 0–4 are developed and examined in relation to state overall population size, the racial/ethnic composition of states, as well other state characteristics thought to be related to Census undercounts. Then a similar analysis is provided for counties.

5.2 Methodology and Data Sources for State-Level Analysis

The methodology used for state Population Estimates is very similar to that used for DA. Both can be described as using a cohort-component approach where each component of population changes (births, deaths and net migration) is estimated separately for each birth cohort. The biggest difference between the national DA and the state Population Estimates is the inclusion of migration across states. Migration between states is captured in the Census Bureau administrative records technique that uses federal tax records to estimate such migration (U.S. Census Bureau 2012b).

Data from the 2010 American Community Survey indicate that 89 % of the population age 0–4 were living in the same state where they were born. Therefore, the overwhelming majority of children age 0–4 estimated in each state come from births in that state. The heavy reliance on birth certificate data and the high quality of birth certificate data provide a strong foundation for state Population Estimates for the population age 0–4.

The state Population Estimates are derived using the formula in Eq. 5.1, which is taken from U.S. Census Bureau (2012a, b);

$$P1 = P0 + B - D + NDM + NIM \qquad (5.1)$$

where

P1   Population at the end of the year
P0   Population at the beginning of the year
B   Births during the year
D   Deaths during the year
NDM   Net domestic migration during the year
NIM   Net International Migration during the year.

The estimated undercounts and overcounts shown here also include errors in the population estimates. However, since the mean absolute percent error for state Population Estimates is on the order of 1 % (Yowell and Devine 2013) and the average state net undercount for the population 0–4, is around 3.5 %, the bulk of the difference appears to be the net undercount rather than the estimation error. The 1 % error noted above is for the total population, not the 0–4 population, but it is the best estimate available for the likely accuracy for the 0–4 population.

In the remainder of this Chapter, the differences between the Census counts and Population Estimates are shown as the Census count *minus* the estimate. This is consistent with the convention used by Velkoff (2011). This calculation is sometimes labeled "net Census coverage error" in other research. A negative number implies a net undercount and a positive number implies a net overcount. I chose to use the net Census coverage error because I feel having an undercount reflected by a negative number is more intuitive and is consistent with the presentation of 2010 DA analysis by Velkoff (2011).

In converting the differences between Census counts and DA estimates to percentages, the difference is divided by the DA estimate. Estimates are shown rounded to the nearest thousand for readability.

5.2.1 The Data

The Vintage 2010 State Population Estimates used here are taken from the Census Bureau's file labeled "Annual State Resident Population Estimates for 5 Race Groups (5 Race Alone or in Combination Groups) by Age, Sex, and Hispanic Origin: April 1, 2000 to July 1, 2010." The file is also denoted as "SC-EST2010-ALLDATA5." The file was released March 2012 and it is available on the Census Bureau's website.

These estimates include the results of special Censuses and successful local challenges during the previous decade. This file contains yearly estimates for 2000 through 2010, but only the estimates from April 1, 2010, for the population age 0–4 are used in this study.

The data from the 2010 U.S. Census are taken from Table QT-P1 in Summary File 1. The data were obtained through American Factfinder available on the Census Bureau's website. The data for the total population and for the population age 0–4 were taken from this file.

The District of Columbia was not included in the state analysis for two reasons. First, The District of Columbia does not operate like a state. Demographically and governmentally, the District of Columbia is more like a large city than a state. Second, the net undercount rate of young children for the District of Columbia is an outlier with respect to state undercount rates for the population age 0–4. The net undercount rate for the District of Columbia was 16.2 %, while the highest net undercount rate for age 0–4 in any state was 10.2 % in Arizona.

Table 5.1 provides national data from the U.S. Census Bureau's Vintage 2010 Population Estimates, the U.S. Census Bureau's May 2012 Demographic Analysis (DA) release, and the 2010 U.S. Decennial Census. For the total population the figures from the three sources are remarkably similar. In reality, the similarities across all three sources for the total population are the product of large counter-balancing differences among age groups.

For the population age 0–4, the DA estimates and the Vintage 2010 Population Estimates are very similar (21,263,000 for the Population Estimate and 21,171,000 for the May 2012 revised DA estimate). More importantly for this paper, both the DA estimate and the Population Estimate figures are substantially higher than the 2010 U.S. Census count (20,201,000). The difference between the DA estimate and the U.S. Census count is 4.6 % for the population age 0–4 and the difference between the Vintage 2010 Population Estimate and the U.S. Census count is 5.0 %. Both the DA estimates and the Vintage 2010 Population Estimates indicate there was a net undercount of about one million children age 0–4.

Table 5.1 Difference between vintage 2010 population estimates, May 2012 DA estimates, and 2010 U.S. census counts by age

(Figures in 1000)		
	All ages	Age 0–4
Population figures		
Population estimates[a]	308,450	21,263
May 2012 DA[b]	308,346	21,171
Census counts[c]	308,746	20,201
Numeric differences		
Census—population estimates	296	−1062
Census—DA	400	−970
Population estimates—DA	104	92
Percentage differences		
(Census—population estimates)/population estimates	0.1	−5
(Census—DA)/DA	0.1	−4.6
(Population estimates—DA)/DA	0	0.4

[a]Vintage 2010 Population Estimate Program (PEP) results for 4/1/2010
[b]U.S. Census Bureau, Population Division, 2010 Demographic Analysis Released May 2012
[c]2010 U.S. Census Summary File 1, Table DP-1 Profile of General Population and Housing Characteristics

The consistency between the national population DA estimates and the corresponding Vintage 2010 State Population Estimates at the national level suggests the Vintage 2010 Population Estimates are likely to be useful for estimating the distribution of the national undercount of the population age 0–4 among the states.

The main reason the Vintage 2010 Population Estimates differ slightly from the 2010 DA estimates is the fact that the DA estimates issued in May 2012 used updated vital events data for 2008, 2009, and the first quarter of 2010. When the Vintage 2010 Population Estimates were issued, the Census Bureau had to estimate the number of births and deaths in 2008, 2009 and the first quarter of 2010 because the empirical data was not yet available from the National Center for Health Statistics. By the time the revised DA estimates were issued in May 2012, the final figures for births and deaths in 2008, 2009 and the first quarter of 2010 were available from the National Center for Health Statistics. The fact that the observed figures for births (used in preparing the 2010 DA estimates released May 2012) were lower than the estimated figures used to prepare the Vintage 2010 Population Estimates, results in the DA estimates being slightly lower than the Vintage 2010 Population Estimates. This results in the Population Estimates providing slightly higher national net undercount rates than DA. But this difference is relatively minor; a 4.6 % net undercount for DA compared to a 5.0 % net undercount for the Population Estimates. Either estimate shows young children had the highest net undercount rate of any age group, by far.

5.3 State-Level Results

Table 5.2 provides several summary measures of differences between the Vintage 2010 Population Estimates and the 2010 U.S. Census counts for state populations age 0–4. For the population age 0–4, the mean difference is −21,114. In relative terms, the mean difference was −3.4 % for the population age 0–4.

Some of the positive and negative differences may cancel each other out in calculating the mean, so it is useful to examine the size of absolute differences. This provides a measure of the size of difference between Census Counts and Population Estimates regardless of direction of the difference. The mean *absolute numeric* difference was 21,176 for the population aged 0–4 and the relative absolute difference was 3.5 %. Since 46 of the 50 states had net undercounts for the population age 0–4 it is not surprising that the numeric mean and the mean of absolute values are similar for young children.

The average state had a net undercount rate of 3.4 % for the population age 0–4, which is substantially less than the national net undercount rate (5.0 % for the Vintage 2010 Population Estimates and 4.6 % based on DA). This indicates that the national undercount for the population age 0–4 is not distributed evenly across the states but is driven by larger errors in large states. This point will be examined in more detail later in this Chapter.

Table 5.3 shows the numeric and percent differences between the Vintage 2010 State Population Estimates and the 2010 U.S. Census counts for the population age 0–4 for each state, developing by subtracting the state estimate from the Census counts.

The data in Table 5.3 indicate that the national undercount rate for the population age 0–4 (5.0 %) masks striking differences across the states. Differences between the 2010 U.S. Census counts and the Vintage 2010 State Population Estimates for age 0–4 range from a net undercount of 10.2 % in Arizona to a 2.1 % net overcount in North Dakota. There were 12 states with net undercounts of 5 % or more.

In population terms, Table 5.3 shows the differences between the 2010 U.S. Census counts and the Vintage 2010 State Population Estimates for age 0–4 range from a net undercount of 210,125 in California to a net overcount of 906 in North Dakota. There are 26 states where the difference between the Vintage 2010 Population estimate and the 2010 Census count for the population age 0–4 was more than 10,000.

Table 5.2 Summary table of *state* differences (census minus population estimates) between Vintage 2010 population estimates and 2010 census count for population age 0–4

Mean numerical difference	−21,114
Mean percent difference	−3.4
Number of states with a net overcount	4
Number of states with a net undercount	46
Mean absolute numeric difference	21,176
Mean absolute percentage difference	3.5

The net undercount of young children is geographically pervasive at the state level. Only four states (North Dakota, Vermont, Montana, and Wyoming) had a net overcount.

There are no standard errors or other measures of uncertainty attached to the Population Estimates or the Census counts, so one cannot employ traditional statistical significance testing. However, in the DA release of December 2010 the Census Bureau offered results for five different DA scenarios to illustrate the uncertainty surrounding the DA estimates. The results of the five scenarios for the population age 0–4, ranged from a low of 21,181,000 to high of 21,265,000. In percentage terms, the difference between the lowest estimate and the highest estimate is 0.4 %. This provides at least one guide to expected errors in the DA estimates.

When state differences between Population Estimates and 2010 U.S. Census counts are compared to the national difference (5.0 %) only four states (Colorado, Delaware, Massachusetts and Mississippi) are within 0.4 percentage points of the national rate. Moreover, only eleven states have a net undercount rate within one percentage point of the national net undercount rate for the population age 0–4. There are only two states (Maine and Wyoming) where the net undercount rate for the population age 0–4 are within 0.4 % points of zero. This suggests significant real variation across the states in the net undercount of the population age 0–4. It also indicates that the national net undercount rate for the population age 0–4 tells us very little about the net undercount rate of young children in most states.

It should be noted that the state-wide net undercount rates examined here reflect significant differences across sub-state areas. In many states, the state figure was a product of net undercounts for young children in large counties and net overcounts in smaller counties. There were 13 states where large counties (populations of 250,000 or more) accounted for all of the net undercount for age 0–4 in the state. This point will be pursued later in this Chapter.

5.4 Characteristics Associated with State Net Undercount Rates for Population Age 0–4

Data presented in the previous section make it clear that the net Census coverage rates for the population age 0–4 vary substantially across the states. In this section, I examine several state characteristics to see which ones are most highly correlated with the net Census coverage rates for young children. While correlation is not the same as causation, finding out which characteristics are most highly correlated with state differences in net undercount of age 0–4 will shed light on what are the most likely causes of the net undercount for young children, or perhaps identify which factors are not likely to be causally related to the net undercount of young children.

Table 5.3 State 2010 census counts minus Vintage 2010 population estimates for the population age 0–4

	Vintage 2010 population estimate program	2010 census counts	Numeric difference (census − estimates)	Percent difference [(census − estimates)/ estimates] * 100
Alabama	317,716	304,957	−12,759	−4
Alaska	54,888	53,996	−892	−1.6
Arizona	507,581	455,715	−51,866	−10.2
Arkansas	204,509	197,689	−6820	−3.3
California	2,741,458	2,531,333	−210,125	−7.7
Colorado	362,049	343,960	−18,089	−5
Connecticut	208,901	202,106	−6795	−3.3
Delaware	59,098	55,886	−3212	−5.4
Florida	1,163,423	1,073,506	−89,917	−7.7
Georgia	741,568	686,785	−54,783	−7.4
Hawaii	90,687	87,407	−3280	−3.6
Idaho	122,759	121,772	−987	−0.8
Illinois	887,157	835,577	−51,580	−5.8
Indiana	444,854	434,075	−10,779	−2.4
Iowa	203,842	202,123	−1719	−0.8
Kansas	207,830	205,492	−2338	−1.1
Kentucky	289,924	282,367	−7557	−2.6
Louisiana	323,481	314,260	−9221	−2.9
Maine	69,779	69,520	−259	−0.4
Maryland	381,289	364,488	−16,801	−4.4
Massachusetts	387,055	367,087	−19,968	−5.2
Michigan	603,376	596,286	−7090	−1.2
Minnesota	362,611	355,504	−7107	−2
Mississippi	221,144	210,956	−10,188	−4.6
Missouri	402,489	390,237	−12,252	−3
Montana	62,143	62,423	280	0.5
Nebraska	134,530	131,908	−2,622	−1.9
Nevada	200,843	187,478	−13,365	−6.7
New Hampshire	71,949	69,806	−2143	−3
New Jersey	555,419	541,020	−14,399	−2.6
New Mexico	153,402	144,981	−8421	−5.5
New York	1,228,587	1,155,822	−72,765	−5.9
North Carolina	657,178	632,040	−25,138	−3.8
North Dakota	43,689	44,595	906	2.1
Ohio	738,494	720,856	−17,638	−2.4
Oklahoma	274,800	264,126	−10,674	−3.9

(continued)

Table 5.3 (continued)

	Vintage 2010 population estimate program	2010 census counts	Numeric difference (census − estimates)	Percent difference [(census − estimates)/ estimates] * 100
Oregon	248,107	237,556	−10,551	−4.3
Pennsylvania	750,821	729,538	−21,283	−2.8
Rhode Island	59,523	57,448	−2075	−3.5
South Carolina	313,334	302,297	−11,037	−3.5
South Dakota	59,998	59,621	−377	−0.6
Tennessee	423,204	407,813	−15,391	−3.6
Texas	2,083,265	1,928,473	−154,792	−7.4
Utah	274,529	263,924	−10,605	−3.9
Vermont	31,699	31,952	253	0.8
Virginia	532,874	509,625	−23,249	−4.4
Washington	457,757	439,657	−18,100	−4
West Virginia	106,985	104,060	−2925	−2.7
Wisconsin	361,741	358,443	−3298	−0.9
Wyoming	40,085	40,203	118	0.3

Sources U.S. Census Bureau (2012a, b)

5.4.1 State Size

Table 5.4 shows the percent difference between 2010 Census counts and Vintage 2010 Population Estimates for population age 0–4 by quintiles of state population size. For all the population size groups, there is a net undercount for the 0–4 population but larger states (in terms of total population) tend to have bigger percentage differences between the 2010 U.S. Census counts and the Vintage 2010 Population Estimates for age 0–4 than smaller states. The collective net undercount for the smallest population quintile was 1.5 % but it was 6.1 % for the largest population quintile.

The five states with the largest net undercounts for children age 0–4, (California, Texas, Florida, New York, and Georgia) had a collective undercount of 579,000 which amounts to 55 % of the total net undercount nationwide for this age group. But only 37 % of the national population age 0–4 live in those five states.

The correlation between the undercount rate for age 0–4 and state population size in the state is −0.54, which underscores the fact that larger states tend to have bigger net undercount rates. Recall undercounts are expressed as a negative number.

The correlation between state population size and net undercount rates for the population age 0–4 is likely related to some of the characteristics of the states that are related to undercounts rather than population size per se. This idea is explored next.

Table 5.4   State differences between 2010 decennial census counts and vintage 2010 population estimates for population age 0–4 by state population quintiles

	Numeric difference between population estimates and census counts (census − estimates)	Percent difference between population estimates and census counts [(census − estimates/ estimates) * 100]
Smallest quintile	−8538	−1.5
Second smallest quintile	−60,414	−3.6
Middle quintile	−88,402	−3.5
Second largest quintile	−193,210	−4
Largest quintile	−705,111	−6.1
Total	−1,055,675	−5

Quintiles are based on total states census counts

5.4.2 Race and Hispanic Origin

Nationally, in 2010, the net undercount rate for Hispanics age 0–4 was 7.5 % and for Blacks Alone or in Combination age 0–4 it was 6.3 % (see Chap. 3). Therefore, one might expect to find that the racial and ethnic composition in a state is related to the net undercount rate for young children. I use the Census counts to measure the distribution of minority groups because the groups are quite small in some states and I feel the counts for Hispanics and Black Alone or in Combination are likely to be more reliable and accurate than Population Estimates for small populations in those states.

Table 5.5 shows correlations between four measures of racial composition and state net undercount rates for the population age 0–4. There is little difference between the correlations based on race/Hispanic origin status of the adult population or the population age 0–4, so only the data for the adult population are shown in Table 5.5.

All of the correlations in Table 5.5 are in the predicted direction, namely, the higher the percentage of minorities the higher the net undercount rate of the population age 0–4. But the magnitudes of the associations vary substantially. All of the correlations in Table 5.5 are statistically significant.

The correlation coefficient between percent Hispanic and the net undercount rates for the population age 0–4 is −0.67, while the correlation between percent Black Alone or in Combination and net undercount rates is −0.35 for the population age 0–4. The higher correlation for Hispanics than for Blacks Alone or in Combination may be due to the fact that Hispanics are a larger population than Black Alone or in Combination and the net undercount rate of young Hispanic children is somewhat higher than that of Black Alone or in Combination. Therefore the impact of Hispanics on a state net undercount rate is likely to be higher than the impact of Blacks Alone or in Combination.

However, when the Black Alone or in Combination population is combined with the Hispanic population to form a broader measure of minority populations,

Table 5.5 Correlations between racial/hispanic composition and net undercount rates for age 0–4 across states

Percent black alone not hispanic age 18+	−0.35
Percent hispanic age 18+	−0.67
Percent black alone not his apnic plus hispanic age 18+	−0.76
Percent minority* age 18+	−0.68

All correlations are statistically significantly different from zero a the 0.05 level

Source Demographic Data from 2010 Census, PL94-171 file

*Minority is defined here as anyone other than Non-Hispanic White Alone

the correlation is higher than either group by itself. For the population age 0–4 the correlation between percent of the population that is Black Alone or in Combination or Hispanic and net undercount is −0.76. I suspect the higher correlation for the combined population of Black Alone or in Combination and Hispanic group reflects the fact that Blacks are the dominant minority population in most of the Southeastern states and Hispanics are the dominant minority population in most Southwestern states. So the combined group covers the largest minority populations in more states.

It is worth noting that the correlation between net Census coverage for age 0–4 and the percent of the state population that is any racial/Hispanic minority (i.e. anything other than Non-Hispanic White Alone) is not as high as the correlation using the combination of Hispanic and Black Alone or in Combination. The correlation between Percent Total Minority and net coverage rate of young children is −0.68. This may be due to the concentration of Asians and American Indians/Alaskan Native in a few states such as Hawaii and Alaska where net undercount rates for the population age 0–4 are low relative to other states.

Many observers feel that the racial differences noted above are the product of differences in factors such as housing and living arrangements rather than race or ethnicity per se. In discussing the undercount of minorities, Schwede et al. (2015, p. 293) state, "Though there is no reason to believe that race or ethnicity in and of itself leads to coverage error, it seems that some underlying variables associated in past studies with undercounting may also be correlated with race (e.g. mobility, complex living situations, and language isolation)." This idea is examined below.

5.4.3 Hard-to-Count Characteristics

Since the 1990s, there has been a sustained effort at the Census Bureau to build a Planning Data Base at the Census tract level which includes information on Hard-to-Count characteristics (Bruce and Robinson 2003, 2007; Bruce et al. 2001; Bruce et al. 2012). Twelve Hard-to-Count factors were used to construct a Hard-to-Count score for each Census tract in the 2000 Census. The twelve characteristics used to calculate a Hard-to-Count scores (Bruce and Robinson 2003) are linked to low mail response rates and the likelihood of being missed in the Census. According to Bruce and Robinson (2003, p. 74), "The variables included in the Planning Database (PDB) were guided by extensive research conducted by the Census Bureau and others to measure the undercount and to identify reasons people are missed…".

In 2014, the Census Bureau released the latest version of the Planning Data Base with data reflecting many of the Hard-to-Count factors (U.S. Census Bureau 2014). Some of the measures are related to housing characteristics and some are related to characteristics of people in households. The variables in the 2014 Planning Data Base also include some of those derived using empirical relationships with the Mail Return Rate (Erdman and Bates 2014).

The correlations between the net undercount rate of the population 0–4 and the twelve Hard-to-Count characteristics are shown in Table 5.6. The measures are listed in order from the most highly correlated to the least highly correlated. Recall that the net undercount rate as measured here is reflected as a negative number so a lower figure reflects a larger net undercount.

Ten of the twelve correlation coefficients in Table 5.6 are in the predicted direction but there are large variations in the size of correlations between the Hard-to-Count measures and the net undercount rates of the population age 0–4.

In general, measures that reflect characteristics of people within a household had higher correlations with the net undercount rate of the population age 0–4 than characteristics of the housing units.

The three measures that are most highly correlated with net undercount among age 0–4 (Linguistic Isolation, Lack of a High School Degree, and Unemployment) are related to characteristics of adults in the household. Since adults in a household typically complete the Census questionnaire, it is not surprising that states where adults are more likely to have problems with filling out for the Census questionnaire have higher net undercount rates for young children.

Percent in Rental Housing and Percent of Housing Units That Are Not Single Detached Units are the housing measures that are most highly correlated (−0.42) with net undercount of the population age 0–4. Percent in Crowded Households also has a moderate correlation (−0.37) with net undercount of 0–4 year olds. Many of these measures are highly correlated with each other so it is difficult to sort out causality.

Four of the twelve correlations are not statistically significantly different from zero. Two measures (Percent of Households Receiving Public Assistance and Percent Vacant Housing Units) actually have a positive correlation with undercount rates of young children at the state level but neither of these correlations is statistically significant. The correlation between net undercount rate for the population age 0–4 and the Percent of the Population That Moved in the Past Year as well as the Percent with No Phone in the Household are in the expected direction, but are not statistically significant.

Some of the weak correlations observed in Table 5.6 may be explained by changes in society since these measures were first identified in the 1990s.

Table 5.6 Correlations between state net undercount rates for population age 0–4 and hard-to-count factors across

	Correlation with state net undercount rate for age 0–4
Percent of households that are linguistically isolated[b]	−0.69[a]
Percent of population age 25+ not high school graduates	−0.58[a]
Percent of people unemployed	−0.57[a]
Percent of occupied housing units that are rental occupied	−0.42[a]
Percent of housing other than single detached units	−0.42[a]
Percent of occupied housing units that are crowded (1.51+ persons per room)	−0.37[a]
Percent of people living below poverty	−0.31[a]
Percent of households that are not husband wife households	−0.27[a]
Percent of occupied housing unit with no phone service	−0.24
Percent of persons age 1+ who moved into unit in last year	−0.18
Percent of households with public assistance income	0.17
Percent vacant housing units	0.15

Source All data are from the 2010 census or the 2010 1-year American Community Survey Estimates
[a]Statistically different from zero at the 0.05 level of significance or higher
[b]Linguistically isolation is measure of households that lack an adult who speaks English well

For example, federal welfare reform that was passed in 1996 changed the major federal program providing cash public assistance as Assistance to Families with Dependent Children was replaced with Temporary Assistance to Needy Families. The changes brought about by the new welfare program (a large decline in the number of families receiving cash public assistance) may mean this measure is no longer a good predictor of Census undercounts. Regarding the lack of a statistically significant correlation between Vacant Housing Units and net undercount rates for age 0–4, it is also important to remember that the 2010 Census took place in the midst of a recession and a "housing crisis." The high level of vacancies which accompanied the housing crisis may have undermined the historic connection between the vacancy rate and Census coverage.

The correlation between the Availability of Phone Service and net undercount rate for population age 0–4 is relatively low at −0.24 and it is not statistically significant. The proliferation of cell phones may have changed the meaning of having a phone at home.

Some of the factors that were not statistically significant at the state level are highly correlated with Mail Return Rates at the Block Group and Tract level. Erdman and Bates (2014) found Percent Moved 2005–2009 as well as Percent in Different House One Year Ago and Percent Vacant units to be important predictors of the Mail Return Rates in analysis related to the 2010 Census.

One other factor that was examined here in addition to traditional Hard-to-Count variables was the Mail Return Rate. The Mail Return Rate is defined by the Census Bureau (2014, p. 36) as:

> The number of mail returns received out of the total number of valid occupied housing units (HUs) in the Mailout/Mailback universe which excludes deleted, vacant, or units identified as undeliverable as addressed.

The correlation between final Mail Return Rates and the net undercount rate for age 0–4 at the state level is +0.50. Recall that net undercount rates are negative numbers so this correlation coefficient indicates the higher the Mail Return Rate the smaller the net undercount for age 0–4. The correlation between the Mail Return Rate and the net undercount rates for age 0–4 is on the same order of magnitude as several of the Hard-to-Count characteristics.

5.5 County Level Undercounts of Young Children

This section examines the net undercount of young children by comparing the Census Bureau's Vintage 2010 Population Estimates for the population age 0–4 to the 2010 Census counts across counties. This analysis focuses on the population age 0–4, because the 2010 DA analysis shows this age group has the largest net undercount of any age group (see Chap. 3).

There are more than 3100 counties in the U.S. but many of them have small populations. In the 2010 Census there were 566 counties with fewer than 500 persons age 0–4 and 1129 with less than one thousand in this age range. Yowell and Devine (2013, Table 7) show the Mean Absolute Percent Error for Population Estimates of the smallest counties is about four times that of the largest counties. Differences between the 2010 Census counts and the Vintage 2010 population estimate for many small counties are fraught with estimation error. Consequently, data for individual small counties are not examined here.

The analysis focuses on groups of counties which is consistent with the advice of Adlakha et al. (2003, p. 34), "In general, the coverage analysis has been carried out for aggregations of counties, because benchmark estimates have certain unmeasured deficiencies, the effect of which is dampened when data are aggregated for higher geographic levels." When counties are grouped together some of the random errors in the estimates for individual counties will cancel each other out. Given the more accurate Population Estimates for large counties (Yowell and Devine 2013), separate analysis is conducted for a subset of large counties.

5.6 The Data

Methods and data used to examine counties are similar to those discussed in the previous section. The Vintage 2010 Population Estimates used here are taken from the Census Bureau's file labeled "Annual County Resident Population Estimates by Age, Sex, Race, and Hispanic Origin: April 1, 2000–July 1, 2010." The file is also denoted as "CC-EST2010-ALLDATA." The file was released March 2012 and it is available on the Census Bureau's website.

This file contains yearly estimates for 2000 through 2010, but only the estimates from April 1, 2010, for the population age 0–4 are used in this study. These estimates include the results of special Censuses and local challenges during the previous decade.

The data from the 2010 Census are taken from Table QT-P1 in Summary File 1. The data were obtained through American Factfinder available on the Census Bureau's website. The data for the total population and for the population age 0–4 were taken from this file.

The 2010 Census results are compared to Vintage 2010 Population Estimates in the 3141 counties or county equivalents (i.e. parishes or independent cities) for which Vintage 2010 Population Estimates were produced. The District of Columbia is treated as a county in this analysis. A few counties are not included in the analysis because they are too small to provide reliable data. Coverage was measured as the Census minus Population Estimates so a negative number means the Census count was less than the Population Estimate. Percentages are derived by dividing the difference by the Population Estimate.

5.7 County-Level Results

Table 5.7 provides several measures of differences between the Vintage 2010 Population Estimates and the 2010 Census counts for counties for the population age 0–4. Across all counties, the mean numerical difference between Census Counts

Table 5.7 County differences between Vintage 2010 population estimates and 2010 census count for population age 0–4

Mean numerical difference	338
Mean percent difference	1.1
Number of counties with a net overcount	1491
Number of counties with a net undercount	1634
Mean absolute numeric difference	1993
Number of counties with absolute numeric difference larger than 5000	57
Mean absolute percentage difference	7.4
Number of counties with absolute percent difference larger than 10 %	674

and the Vintage 2010 Population Estimates for the population age 0–4 was 338. The average county had an overcount of 1.1 % for the population age 0–4. Since this average county overcount is quite different than the national undercount rate (5.0 % based on Vintage 2010 Population Estimates and 4.6 % based on DA) it indicates that the national rate is driven by high net undercount rates in large counties.

Unlike states where almost all of the states (46 of the 50) experienced a net undercount, counties have a more balanced distribution. There were 1634 counties with a net undercount of the population age 0–4 and 1491 counties with a net overcount of the population age 0–4. For sixteen counties the population estimate and the Census count were exactly the same for the population age 0–4.

Because errors in different directions cancel each other out in calculating the mean it is important to look at absolute differences as well. In absolute terms, the mean difference between the county population estimate for age 0–4 and the Census count for that age group was 1993. In percentage terms the average absolute difference was 7.4 %.

5.7.1 Characteristics Associated with County Net Undercount Rates for Population Age 0–4

There is a clear relationship between county size and collective undercount rates with larger counties having the highest undercount rates and smaller counties having net overcounts. Table 5.8 shows the mean percent difference for the smallest counties (less than 5000 people) is a 5.1 % net overcount compared to a 7.8 % net undercount for the largest counties (those of 500,000 or more people).

The correlation between net undercount rate for the population age 0–4 and size of county population (total population) is modest (-0.28). I suspect the correlation coefficient in confounded by the relatively large errors associated with Population Estimates for smaller counties.

Table 5.8 Difference between 2010 census counts and Vintage 2010 population estimates for population age 0–4 by county size

Total population size of county	Number of counties	Aggregate population estimate (in 1000 s)	Aggregate census count (In 1000 s)	Census − estimate (in 1000 s)	Percent difference[a]
Less than 5000	303	48	50	2	5.1
5000–9999	395	181	183	2	1.3
10,000–24,999	845	886	882	−4	−0.5
25,000–49,999	624	1438	1421	−18	−1.2
50,000–99,999	398	1776	1757	−20	−1.1
100,000–499,999	450	6381	6178	−203	−3.2
500,000+	128	10,553	9729	−823	−7.8
Total	3143	21,263	20,201	−1062	−5

[a]Percent calculated on unrounded numbers

Table 5.9 Net undercount of young children in the ten largest counties in 2010

Rank based on total population	County (major city)		Population estimate	Census	Difference (census − estimate)	Percent difference[a]
1	Los Angeles (Los Angeles)	California	719,712	645,793	−73,919	−10.3
2	Cook (Chicago)	Illinois	385,195	342,493	−42,702	−11.1
3	Harris (Houston)	Texas	365,048	336,314	−28,734	−7.9
4	Maricopa (Phoenix)	Arizona	323,013	282,770	−40,243	−12.5
5	San Diego (San Diego)	California	226,006	203,423	−22,583	−10
6	Orange (Anaheim)	California	214,801	191,691	−23,110	−10.8
7	Kings (New York)	New York	199,891	177,198	−22,693	−11.4
8	Miami − Dade (Miami)	Florida	170,662	149,937	−20,725	−12.1
9	Dallas (Dallas)	Texas	223,980	192,838	−31,142	−13.9
10	Queens (New York)	New York	152,336	132,464	−19,872	−13

[a]Percent calculated on unrounded data

Table 5.8 indicates the 128 counties with half a million or more people had a cumulative net undercount of 823,000 persons and a net undercount rate of 7.8 % for the population age 0–4. Thus these 128 counties account for 77 % of the total national net undercount of slightly over one million people age 0–4, even though only 50 % of the national population age 0–4 live in these counties.

Table 5.9 shows the net undercount rates in the ten largest counties in the nation. Nine of the ten largest counties had a net undercount rate for young children of at least 10 %. Harris County, Texas, is the exception with a net undercount rate of 7.9 %. Undercount estimates for individual counties should be viewed cautiously, but the consistently high net undercount rate for all ten large counties in Table 5.9, plus the evidence in Table 5.8, strongly suggest high net undercount rates for the population age 0–4 for the largest counties in the country.

5.7.2 Race and Hispanic Origin DA

This section looks at the relationship between county racial/Hispanic composition and net undercount of the population age 0–4. The first analysis looks at all counties then the analysis is repeated with only the largest counties (population 250,000 or more) where Population Estimates are likely to be more accurate.

Table 5.10 Correlations between racial/ethnic composition of a county and net undercount rates for age 0–4

	All counties	Counties with populations of 250,000 or more
Percent non-hispanic black alone	−0.21	−0.35
Percent hispanic	−0.12	−0.4
Percent non-hispanic black alone + hispanic	−0.25	−0.59
Percent minority (other than non-hispanic white)	−0.25	−0.59

All Correlations in this table are significant at the 0.01 level (2-tailed)

I use the 2010 Census figures for Black Alone, Black Alone or in Combination, total minority population (i.e. anyone who is not Non-Hispanic White) and Hispanics. The data for these populations are taken from the 2010 Census using American Factfinder.

Table 5.10 shows the correlations between four measures of racial/Hispanic composition in a county and the net undercount rate for the population age 0–4. The racial composition is based on the adult population (age 18+) because adults are usually responsible for filling out the Census questionnaire.

For all counties, all the correlations are in the expected direction (negative correlations for every minority group measured) and all of the correlations are statistically significant, but the correlations are relatively modest in size and range from −0.12 to −0.25. The correlation between net undercount rates and the percent Non-Hispanic Black Alone (−0.21) is higher than the correlation between the net undercount rate and Hispanics (−0.12) which is the opposite order of what was found at the state level. The correlations may be confounded by high estimation errors for many individual counties and a very small minority population in many counties.

For the largest counties (those of 250,000 or more people) the correlations are in the predicted direction and statistically significant but higher in magnitude. As with states, there is a higher correlation when Blacks (Alone or in Combination) and Hispanics are combined (−0.59) into one measure of minority population than for either Blacks (−0.35 for Non-Hispanic Black alone) or Hispanics (−0.40).

5.8 Summary

Forty-six of the fifty states experienced a net undercount for the population age 0–4 and 12 states experienced net undercount rates of 5 % of more. At the state level, the net coverage rates for the population age 0–4 in the 2010 U.S. Census varies from a 10.2 % net undercount in Arizona to 2.1 % overcount in North Dakota.

In general, larger states (in population size) had higher net undercount rates than smaller states. The net undercount rates in states are correlated with the size of the Black and/or Hispanic population, although the correlation is much higher for Hispanics than for Blacks.

The relationships between traditional Hard-to-Count characteristics and net undercount rates for the population age 0–4 at the state level vary. Looking across states, the characteristics that are most highly correlated with net undercount rates for age 0–4 are personal characteristics (Linguistic Isolation, Lack of a High School Degree, and Unemployment Rate) rather than housing characteristics.

The data examined here indicate that the national net undercount rate for the population age 0–4 varies substantially across counties. About half of the counties experienced a net undercount and half of the counties experienced a net overcount. Larger counties account for the vast majority of the national net undercount for the population age 0–4. In the 128 largest counties based on total 2010 Census population, there was a net undercount of 823,000 persons age 0–4 which amounts to 77 % of the national undercount of persons age 0–4 even though only 50 % of young children living in these counties. All of the ten largest counties have net undercount rates of 7.9 % or higher for the population age 0–4.

References

Adlakha, A. L., Robinson, J. G., West, K. K., & Bruce, A. (2003). Assessment of consistency of census data with demographic benchmarks at the subnational level. Census 2000 Evaluation 0.20 U.S. Census Bureau.

Bruce, A., Robinson. J. G., & Sanders, M. V. (2001). Hart-to-count scores and broad demographic groups associated with patterns of response rates in census 2000. In *Proceedings of the Social Statistics Section*, American Statistical Association, 2001.

Bruce, A., & Robinson, J. G. (2003). *The planning database: Its development and use as an effective tool in census 2000.* Paper presented at the Annual Meeting of the Southern Demographic Association, Arlington, VA Oct 24.

Bruce, A., & Robinson, J. G. (2007). *Tract-Level planning database with census 2000 census data.* U.S. Census Bureau, Washington, DC.

Bruce, A., Robinson. J. G., & Devine J. E. (2012). A planning database to identify areas that are hard-to-enumerate and hard to survey in the United States. In *Proceedings of the International Conference on Methods for Surveying and Enumerating Hard-to-Reach Populations*, American Statistical Association.

Cohn, D. (2011). State population estimates and census 2010 counts: Did they match? Pew Social and Demographic Trends, Pew Research Center, Washington, DC. January 12.

Darga, K. (1999). *Sampling and the census.* Washington DC: American Enterprise Institute Press.

Davis, S. T. (1994). Evaluation of post census county estimates for the 1980s. *Current Population reports*, (Series P-25, No. 963, U.S. Census Bureau, Washington DC).

Erdman, C., & Bates, N. (2014). *The census bureau mail return rate challenge: Crowdsourcing to development hard-to-count scores.* Washington, DC: U.S Census Bureau.

Felton, G. T. (1986). Evaluation of population estimation procedures for counties: 1980. *Current Population Reports*, (P-25, NO. 984, U.S. Census Bureau, Washington, DC).

Gormley, W. T. (2012). *Voices for children: Rhetoric and public policy.* Washington DC: Brookings Institution Press.

Hill, R. B., & Steffes, R. B. (1973). *Estimating the 1970 census undercount for state and local areas.* Washington, DC: National Urban League.

Isaki, C. T., Schultz, L. K., Smith, P. J., & Diffendal, G. (1985). *Small Area Estimation Research for Census Undercount—Progress Report*. Paper presented at the International Symposium on Small Area Statistics, U.S. Bureau of the Census, Ottawa, Canada, May.

Mayol-Garcia, Y., & Robinson, J. G. (2011). Census 2010 counts compared to the 2010 population estimates by demographic characteristics. Poster presented at the Southern Demographic Association Conference, October, Tallahassee, FL.

O'Hare, W. P. (1988). How to evaluate population estimates. *American Demographics*, 10(1).

O'Hare, W. P. (2013). *Difference between 2010 census counts and Vintage 2010 population estimates for age 0–4 at the state and county level*. Poster presented at the 2013 Annual Conference of the Population Association of America, New Orleans, LA.

O'Hare, W. P. (2014a). *Estimating the net undercount of young children in the 2010 U.S. census at the county level*. Poster presented at the 2014 Population Association of America Conference, Boston, MA. April.

O'Hare, W. P. (2014b). State-level 2010 census coverage rates for young children. *Population Research and Policy Review, 33*(6), 797–816.

O'Hare, W. P. (2014c). Assessing net coverage for young children in the 2010 U.S. decennial census. *International Journal of Population Research*, 2014. http://dx.doi.org/10.1155/2014/671715.

Robinson, J. G., Bashir, A., & Fernandez, E. W. (1993). Demographic analysis as an expanded program for early coverage evaluation of the 2000 census. 1993 Annual Research Conference, March 21–24, Arlington VA.

Robinson, J. G., & Kobilaric, E. L. (1995). Identifying differential undercounts at local geographic levels: A targeting database approach. Paper presented at the Annual Meeting of the Population Association of America, San Francisco.

Schwede, L., Terry, R., & Hunter, J. (2015). Ethnographic evaluations on coverage of hard-to-count minority in the US decennial censuses. In R. Tourangeau, B. Edwards, T. P. Johnson, K. M. Wolter, & N. Bates (Eds.), *Hart-to-survey populations* (pp. 293–315). Cambridge, England: Cambridge University Press.

Siegel, J. S., Passel, J. S., Rives, N. W., & Robinson, J. G. (1977). Developmental estimates of the coverage of the population of states in the 1970 census: Demographic analysis. *Current Population Reports*, Special Studies, (Series P-23, No. 65), December, 1977.

U.S. Census Bureau. (2012a). *Documentation for the revised 2010 demographic analysis middle series estimates*. Washington, DC: U.S. Census Bureau.

U.S. Census Bureau. (2012b). *Population estimation methodology*. U.S. Census Bureau, Washington, DC.

U.S. Census Bureau. (2014). *Planning database with 2010 census and 2008-2012 American community survey data: At the tract level*. U.S. Census Bureau, Washington, DC.

Velkoff, V. (2011). *Demographic evaluation of the 2010 census*. Paper presented at the 2011 Population Association of America annual Conference, Washington, DC.

Yowell, T., & Devine, J. (2013). Evaluating current and alternative methods to produce 2010 county population estimates. Population Division Working Paper 100, U.S. Bureau of the Census. Washington DC, July, 2013.

Chapter 6
Coverage of Young Children in the Census: An International Comparative Perspective

Abstract Review of census results from several other countries show that a net undercount of young children is very common. Only one of the countries examined here did not have a net undercount for young children. Like the U.S., younger children experienced a higher net undercount that older children in most countries examined here. Unlike the U.S., where the net undercount rate for young children (age 0–4) is higher than any other age group, in most countries young adults are the age group with the highest net undercount rate.

Keywords International · Census coverage

This chapter provides an examination of the undercount of young children in Censuses across multiple countries. The analysis here is framed by comparing the results in other countries to the key results in the U.S. Three specific questions are addressed related to patterns seen in the U.S. Census:

1. Is a net undercount rate (as opposed to a net overcount) for young children common?
2. Is the net undercount rate for young children commonly higher than the net undercount rate for older children?
3. Is the net undercount rate for young children commonly higher than the net undercount rate for any other age group?

The Censuses examined here were conducted under a variety of conditions and use a variety of methods to evaluate results, but it is not my intention to examine the methods used. There are several good descriptions of international approaches to measuring Census coverage (Elkin et al. 2012; Kerr 1998; Bryan and Heuser 2004). The point here is to see if the patterns found in a variety of other countries are consistent with the results of the U.S. Census.

The comparisons here are driven largely by the data available from the respective countries. Many countries do not conduct systematic assessments of their Censuses and/or they do not make them publically, or at least easily, available. In addition, I was limited to studies reported in English. Most reports on Census undercounts

© The Author(s) 2015
W.P. O'Hare, *The Undercount of Young Children in the U.S. Decennial Census*,
SpringerBriefs in Population Studies, DOI 10.1007/978-3-319-18917-8_6

provide only limited detail with respect to net undercount by age. So some coverage reports were not relevant for this study because they do not show data for young children. In addition components of net coverage (omissions and erroneous inclusions) are seldom reported so the analysis here focuses on net coverage errors.

The collection of countries examined here is certainly not a representative sample, but the sizable number of countries included here and the fact that they reflect different methods for Census-taking and for evaluation make the findings more robust. In addition, they represent many different levels of socioeconomic development, different cultures, and different Census-taking traditions.

A few previous studies have compared multiple countries in terms of Census coverage. For example, Simpson and Middleton (1997) examined the results of Censuses from Australia, Britain, Canada and the United States to find characteristics of non-response that are common among those countries. The results from Simpson and Middleton list six characteristics associated with high non-response rates across the countries;

- Single and divorced males
- Recent migrants
- Unemployed
- Minority ethnic groups
- Private renters
- Those who share a dwelling with other households or with a business

None of these reflect children or characteristics closely related to children.

I found only one study containing international comparisons related to the coverage of children in multiple Censuses. After assessing the coverage of children in the 2000 Chinese Census, Anderson (2004) examined selected Census results for children from Australia, New Zealand, South Africa, Soviet Union and the United States and generally finds net undercounts of young children in all of the countries examined. The paper by Anderson provides several tables with Census coverage data on young children as well as other age groups but the text section of the paper devotes only three paragraphs to young children. Some of the results shown in Andersons' study are repeated and updated here.

6.1 Is a Net Undercount Rate (As Opposed to a Net Overcount) for Young Children Common?

Table 6.1 provides data on net undercount rates for children in the six countries. For every country except New Zealand, data are reported for age 0–4. New Zealand reports age 0–14. In a few cases data were only reported by sex, not for the total population, so I use the undercount estimates for males and females separately.

In every one of the 22 examples in Table 6.1 there was a net undercount of children age 0–4, but the rate varied over time and across countries. The minimum

Table 6.1 Net undercount rates for children and other age groups from selected countries

New Zealand	Age 0–14			Age 15–29
1996	−1.7			−2.5
2001	−2.7			−3.1
2006	−1			−4.1
South Africa	Age 0–4	Age 5–9	Age 10–14	Age 20–29
2011	−15.1	−11.4	−11.1	−18.1
Canada	Age 0–4	Age 5–14	Age 15–17	Age 20–24
1976	−2.3	−1.2	−2	−5.3
1981	−1.2	−1.2	−3	−5.5
1986	−2.1	−2.1	−3.6	−8.7
1991	−3.6	−2.5	−3.8	−8.2
1996	−2.9	−1.5	−3.5	−8
2001	−4.4	−2.9	−4.4	−9.9
2006	−4.1	−3.1	−4.4	−10.5
2011	−3.4	−2.7	−2.7	
Australia	Age 0–4	Age 5–9	Age 10–14	Age 20–24
1976 Males	−2.9	−2	−1.8	−5.6
1976 Females	−3.1	−1.7	−1.5	−3.9
1991	−1.6	−1.4	−1.1	−3.6
1996	−1.4	−1.4	−1	−3.5
2001	−1.5	−1.5	−1.2	−3.1
2006	−3.4	−2.4	−2.1	−6.8
2011	−1.2	−1.5	−0.4	−6.9
England and Wales	Age 0–4	Age 5–9	Age 10–14	Age 20–24
2011	−9.6	−8	−6.6	−10.9
2001 Males	−9	−7	−7	−13
2001 Females	−9	−7	−7	−11
1991 Males	−5.5	−4	−3.5	−11
1991 Females	−5	−2.5	−2	−5
France	Age 0–4	Age 5–9	Age 10–14	Age 20–24
2006	−1.9	1.8	1.9	−0.6

For consistency, net undercounts are denoted with a negative sign
Sources See Appendix

value seen was −1.2 % net undercount rate in Australia in 2011 and Canada in 1981. The maximum value was −15.1 % undercount in South Africa in 2011.

The mean for all 22 net undercount rates for the population age 0–4 in Table 6.1 is −4.2 %, but it should be noted that this mean includes South Africa where the net undercount rate for young children was 15.1 %. In the three cases for New Zealand where only data for age 0–14 are available, all three cases show a net undercount for children.

Table 6.2 shows data from an article by Goodkind (2011) containing net undercount rates of young children from eleven Asian countries. In 10 of the 11 countries in Table 6.2, there was a net undercount of children age 0–4. The Census coverage rates for age 0–4 range from a 15.9 % net undercount in Mongolia to a 0.3 % net overcount in Taiwan. The mean for the 11 net undercount rates for age 0–4 shown in Table 6.2 is 7.3 % Seven of the eleven countries had net undercount rates for age 0–4 of 5 % or higher.

Table 6.3 provides nine estimates for undercounts of children age 0–4 in various Chinese Censuses from a couple of different sources. In every case, there was a net undercount for children age 0–4 and in some cases the estimated net undercounts were very high. For example, one estimate for the net undercount of children age 0–4 in the 2000 Census was 26.2 %.

The evidence presented here indicates that a net undercount of young children is common in many countries around the world. For the all of the examples examined in Tables 6.1, 6.2 and 6.3 (including age 0–14 in New Zealand and age 0–9 in China) there is only one instance (Taiwan in 2000) where there was a net overcount of young children, and that net overcount was very small.

In addition to the systematic data shown in Tables 6.1, 6.2, and 6.3 there are a few other examples in the literature of Census evaluations which show net undercounts of young children. Recent evaluation of the Philippine Census in 2000 and 2010 found a net undercount of young children (Cruz et al. 2014). Depending on the method used the net undercount for the population age 0–4 was in the range of 5–10 %. By comparing Census results to school enrollment, Anderson and Silver (1985) concluded that there was an under-enumeration of children and adolescents in the 1959 and 1970 Soviet Censuses. Similar results were reported by Baldwin (1973). Desplanques (2008) reviews data from 1990 to 2007 comparing

Table 6.2 Census coverage rates for young children in selected Asian countries

	Date	Coverage rate for age 0–4[a]	Coverage rate for age 5–9[a]
Mongolia	2000	−15.9	−7.1
Indonesia	2000	−13.4	−7
Cambodia	1998	−11.4	−3.9
Vietnam	1999	−10.1	−0.1
Philippines	1995	−7.9	−3.6
Sri Lanka	2001	−7.6	−5.3
Thailand	2000	−5.3	−2.1
Macau	2001	−3.9	1.1
South Korea	2000	−3.6	−3.3
Japan	2000	−2.3	−1.2
Taiwan	2000	0.3	−0.3
Mean		−7.4	−3.0

[a]Negative numbers indicate an implied undercount and positive numbers indicate an implied overcount

Source Authors reconfiguration of data in an article by Goodkind (2011)

Table 6.3 Estimated net census undercounts of children in China	Date	Coverage rate for age 0–4	Coverage rate for age 5–9
	1982	−4.2	0.4
	1982	−7	0.8
	1990	−4.8	−2.1
	1990	−8	−4.2
	2000	−26.2	−12.1
	2000	−17.2	−4.4
	2000	−19.1	−11.9
	1990		
	Male	6.2	
	Female	7.5	

Sources Goodkind (2011) and Cai and Lavely (2003)

Census results and vital records for people born in metropolitan areas of France. In general his data show that younger children typically have a net undercount rate between 2 and 6 %. In reviewing the 2001 South African Census figures for a selected rural geographic area within country, Nyirenda et al. (no date, p. 1) conclude, "Despite the almost universal participation rates of the studied population in the longitudinal demographic surveillance, we still find evidence of under enumeration of children."

In many instances, infants face high odds of being undercounted. For example the 1976 New Zealand Census, Yurjevich (1982) estimated that 3 % of those less than one year of age were missed. Two somewhat dated reports from the U.S. Census Bureau (1944, 1953) also indicate a high net undercount of infants in the past.

The pattern seen in Censuses from a wide variety of countries is similar to the pattern seen in the U.S. In almost every case examined here, the population age 0–4 had a net Census undercount.

6.2 Is the Net Undercount Rate for Young Children Commonly Higher Than the Net Undercount Rate for Older Children?

Data in Table 6.1 shows that in most cases the net undercount rate for those age 0–4 is higher than that for older children. In Table 6.1 there are undercounts rates available for age 5–9, age 10–14, age 15–17 and age 5–14 to compare with the net undercount of the population age 0–4. There are 44 situations where the net undercount rate of young children can be compared to older children. In 33 out of the 44 comparisons, the net undercount rate for young children is as high or higher than the net undercount rate for older children.

In Table 6.2 there are 11 sets of net undercount rates for age 0–4 and 5–9 in 11 Asian countries. In every one of the countries, except Taiwan, the net undercount for children age 0–4 was higher than the net undercount for children age 5–9. For data presented in Table 6.2, the mean net undercount rate for age 0–4 was 7.4 % and for age 5–9 it was 3.0 %.

The data for China shown in Table 6.3 provide seven examples with net undercount data for age 0–4 and age 5–9. In every case, the net undercount for age 0–4 is higher than the net undercount rate for age 5–9.

The findings above are consistent with the observations of others. For example, after reviewing data from several different Censuses, Anderson (2004, p. 10) concludes "Young children are less reliably captured than children in their early teens, for both sexes." Desplanques (2008, Fig. 2) reviews data from 1990 to 2007 comparing Census results and vital records for people born in metropolitan areas of France. In general his data show that younger children typically had slightly higher net undercount rates than older children. After reviewing census results from several countries, Simpson and Middleton (1997, p. 4) conclude, "The following features are apparent. Young children are less reliably captured than children in their early teens for both sexes."

Evidence cited above indicates that young children (age 0–4) have higher net undercount rates than older children (age 5–17) in most Censuses results examined here.

6.3 Is the Net Undercount Rate for Young Children Higher Than the Net Undercount Rate for Any Other Age Group?

The net undercount rate for young children the 2010 U.S. Census is twice as high as any other age group. In that regard the United States is an outlier. Typically young children do not have the highest net undercount rate of any age group.

Table 6.1 shows net undercount rates for young children and for young adults in different countries. The exact age of young adults varies by country. For all of the countries except New Zealand and South Africa data are shown for age 20–24. In every case where data are available for both age groups, the net undercount of people age 20–24 is higher than that of age 0–4. In New Zealand the comparison is between age 0 and 14 and age 15–29. In every case those age 15–29 have a higher net undercount rate than those age 0–14. In South Africa the young adult population is age 20–29, and the population age 20–29, has a higher net undercount rate than the population age 0–4.

The data above is consistent with many observations about Census-taking. In a comparative review of Censuses from several countries, Anderson (2004, p. 10) concludes "Young adult men were hardest to enumerate." A report on the 2001 Australia Census by the Australian Bureau of Statistics (2003, p. 20) concludes,

"The likelihood of enumerating a person in the Census is closely linked to the age and sex of that person. As has been observed in previous Censuses in Australia, as well as in Censuses overseas, young adult males are the group least likely to be enumerated in the Census." In preparing for the 2011 Census in Great Britain, the population of adults age 20–29 was categorized as having a high likelihood of being Hard-To-Count, while they note the 2001 Census nonresponse rate for this group was 11.9 % (Abbott and Compton 2015). Simpson and Middleton (1997) conclude that, "Young adult men are the hardest group to enumerate."

The evidence suggests that the U.S. is an outlier in terms of young children having the highest net undercount rate of any age group. For most countries examined here, young adults have the highest net undercount rate.

6.4 Summary

Like the U.S. experience, net Census undercounts are seen for young children in almost every country examined here. Generally young children have higher net undercount rates that older children in the Censuses examined here.

Unlike the U.S. experience, in most of the Censuses examined here young children are not the age group with the highest net undercount rates. The highest rates are typically for young adults, especially young adult males.

Given the relatively pervasive patterns seen among the countries studied here, the topic of net undercount of children merits further study in additional countries. The strong patterns observed in this collection of countries suggest the findings shown here are likely to be found elsewhere as well.

Appendix

Sources for the data shown in Table 6.1.

A.1 Canada

Dolson, D. (2013). *Differential coverage error for young children in the Canadian census.* Presentation at the Joint Statistical Meeting, Montreal, Canada August (Authors calculation from Chart in Dolsons presentation).

Statistics Canada. (2004). *2001 Census Technical Report: Coverage* (Statistics Canada Catalogue No. 92-394-X). Ottawa, Canada.

Statistics Canada. (2010). *2006 Census Technical Report: Coverage* (Statistics Canada Catalogue No. 92-567-X). Ottawa, Canada. (Table 11.2, p. 102).

A.2 New Zealand

Statistics New Zealand. (2007). *A Report on the 2006 Post-enumeration survey.* Table 1, Wellington, NZ (Table 1, p. 11).
Anderson, B. A. (2004). *Undercount in China's 2000 census in comparative perspective* (PSC Research Report No. 04-565). Population Studies Center, University of Michigan, Ann Arbor, MI (Fig. 11, p. 9).

A.3 South Africa

Statistics South Africa. (1993). *Office of Population Censuses and Surveys.*
Statistics South Africa. (2012). *Post-enumeration survey: Results and methodology* (Report No. 03-01-46). Pretoria, South Africa (Table 11).

A.4 England

Office of National Statistics. (2012). *Response rates in the 2011 Census, London.*
Office of National Statistics. (2005). *Census 2001; quality report for England and Wales, London, England.*

A.5 France

Desplanques, G. (2008). Strengths and uncertainties of the French annual census surveys. *Population-E*, 415–440.

A.6 Australia

Anderson, B. A. (2004). *Undercount in China's 2000 census in comparative perspective* (PSC Research Report No. 04-565). Population Studies Center, University of Michigan, Ann Arbor, MI. (Fig. 9, p. 8).
Australian Bureau of Statistics. (1991). *Census of population and housing, census 91. Data quality—Undercount* (Report No. 2940.0). Canberra.
Australian Bureau of Statistics. (1995). *Census of population and housing, 6 August 1991 census 91. Data quality—Undercount.* Canberra, Australia.
Australia Bureau of Statistics. (1997). *Census of population and housing: Data quality—Undercount; 1996.* Canberra, Australia.
Australian Bureau of Statistics. (1999). *Demography working paper 1999/4– Measuring census undercount in Australia and New Zealand Report 3118.0.* Canberra.

Australian Bureau of Statistics. (2003). *Information paper: Census of population and housing data quality—Undercount* (Report No. 2940.0). Dennis Trewin, Canberra.

Australian Bureau of Statistics. (2007). *Census of population and housing—Undercount 2006* (Paper 2940.0). Canberra, Australia.

Australian Bureau of Statistics. (2012). *Census of population and housing—Details of undercount 2011* (Report 2940.0). Canberra.

Australian Bureau of Statistics. (2012). *Census of population and housing—Details of undercount 2011* (Report 2940.0). Canberra, Australia.

Australian Bureau of Statistics. (2012). *Information paper: Measuring net undercount in the 2011 Population Census* (Report No. 2940.55.001). Canberra.

References

Abbott, O., & Compton, G. (2015). Counting and estimating hard-to-survey populations. In R. Tourangeau, B. Edwards, T. P. Johnson, K. M. Wolter, & N. Bates (Eds.), *Hard-to-survey populations* (pp. 58–81). Cambridge: Cambridge University Press.

Anderson, B. A., & Silver, B. D. (1985). Estimating census undercount from school enrollment data: An application to the soviet censuses on 1959 and 1970. *Demography, 22*(2), 289–308.

Anderson, B. A. (2004). *Undercount in China's 2000 census in comparative perspective.* PSC Research Report, no. 04-565, Population Studies Center, University of Michigan, Ann Arbor, MI.

Australian Bureau of Statistics. (2003). Information Paper: Census of Population and Housing Data Quality-Undercount, 2940.0, Dennis Trewin, Canberra.

Baldwin, G., (1973). *Estimates and projections of the population of the U.S.S.R. by age and sex: 1950-2000.* U.S. Department of Commerce, International Population Reports, Series P-91, No. 24. Washington DC.

Bryan, T., & Heuser, R. (2004). Collection and processing of demographic data. In J. S. Siegel & D. A. Swanson (Ed.), *The methods and materials of demography* (2nd ed.). Elsevier Academic Press, pp. 43–64.

Cai, Y., & Lavely, W. (2003). China's missing girls: numerical estimates and effects on population growth. *The China Review, 3*(2 Fall).

Cruz, G. C., Cruz, J. P., & Kabamalan, M. M. (2014). *Assessing and adjusting the 2000 Philippine census population count.* Poster Presented at the Population Association of America Conference, Boston, MA. May 1–3.

Desplanques, G. (2008). Strengths and uncertainties of the french annual census surveys. *Population–E*, pp. 415–440.

Elkin, M., Dent, P., & Rahman, N. (2012). *A review of international approaches to estimating and adjusting for under- and over-coverage.* United Kingdom, London: Office of National Statistics.

Goodkind, D. (2011). Child underreporting, fertility and sex ratio imbalance in China. *Demography, 48*, 291–316.

Kerr, D. (1998). *A review of procedures for estimating the net undercount of censuses in Canada, the United States, Britain, and Australia.* Ottawa, Canada: Statistics Canada.

Nyirenda, M., Hosehood, V., & Moultrie, T. A., (no date). *Population modelling for a small area: a comparative analysis of census and demographic surveillance system data in South Africa.* African Centre for Health and Population Studies, KwaZulu Natal, South Africa.

Simpson, L., & Middleton, E. (1997). *Who is missed by a national census? A review of empirical results from Australia, Britain, Canada, and the USA.* UK: The Cathie Marsh Centre for Census and Survey Research, University of Manchester.

U.S. Census Bureau. (1944). *Population differential fertility: 1940 and 1910; Standardized fertility rates and reproduction rates*. Appendix A, Completeness of Enumeration of Children Under 5 Years Old in the U.S. Census of 1940 and 1910, 1940 Census, U.S. Census Bureau, Washington, DC.

U.S. Census Bureau. (1953). *Infant enumeration study*. 1950 Procedural studies of the 1950 Censuses, No. 1, Washington, DC.

Yurjevich, M. (1982). Underenumeration of babies in the 1976 census of population and dwellings. *Demographic Bulletin, 4*(2) (Department of Statistics, Wellington)

Chapter 7
Potential Explanations for the High Net Undercount of Young Children in the U.S. Census

Abstract There is a dearth of studies focused on the reasons for the high net undercount of young children in the U.S. Census. Several different potential ideas that might account for the high net undercount of young children are examined and where available, relevant data are examined. One key distinction is the portion of the net undercount of young children due to whole households being missed in the Census compared to people being missed because they were left off question-naires that were return.

Keyword Explanations for undercount

Despite the evidence regarding the continuing problem of high net undercounts of young children in the U.S. Census there is a dearth of ideas in the demographic literature about why young children have such high net undercount rates. In one of the few papers focused on the undercount of children in the U.S. Census, West and Robinson (1999, p. 7) conclude, "There have not been systematic attempts to look at reasons for undercounting children." The conclusion reached by West and Robinson in 1999 is still true today. Citations in the report of the Census Bureau's Task Force on the Undercount of Young Children (Griffin 2014) reflect the paucity of previous work focused on reasons for the high net undercount of young children. This chapter is an attempt to fill that gap in the literature.

This issue is complicated because it involves many potential factors and some of the evidence is inconsistent if not contradictory. In addition, it is important to recognize that ideas about why young children have a high net undercount must not just explain why young children are missed, but why they are missed at a much higher rate than other age groups, including older children.

There are numerous reports that address the issue of why people are missed (omissions) or counted twice (erroneously enumerations) in the Census (de la Puente 1993; Martin and de la Puente 1993; Simpson and Middleton 1997; Schwede and Terry 2013; West and Fein 1990) but I am not aware of any publica-tion which focuses on the reasons young children have a high net undercount other than the report from the U.S. Census Bureau's Task Force on the Undercount of Young Children (Griffin 2014).

This chapter identifies several possible reasons for the high net undercount rate of young children in the U.S. Census and examines statistical data related to many of the ideas. Some of the ideas examined here reflect broad factors (like the characteristics of households and living arrangement of young children) and some reflect narrow factors (like the age imputation algorithm used by the Census Bureau). The Chapter draws heavily on a report by the U.S. Census Bureau's Task Force on the Undercount of Young Children (Griffin 2014).

The information shown here should be seen as the first step in an on-going exploration of reasons why there is a high net undercount of young children. Hopefully future research will add information to better assess the ideas presented here and/or identify other potential reasons to explain the high net undercount of young children.

Given the size and complexity of the Census-taking operation, it is unlikely that there is one simple reason for the high net undercount of young children. However, given the significant and growing nature of this problem it is important for the field to begin developing ideas about why this phenomenon has occurred. Without a clear idea about what causes the high net undercount of young children in the Census, it is unlikely that it can be corrected.

7.1 Potential Explanations for the High Net Undercount Rate of Young Children

Many researchers decompose Census coverage along the lines of Olson (2009) who posits that any omission in the Census-taking process must come from a failure of one of three steps below;

- Failure to enumerate housing unit
- Failure to get a complete and accurate roster of household members
- Failure to get information for a person on the roster

To reconfigure these three reasons for omissions, the first means the household did not get enumerated, and the second and third, means the household was enumerated, but not everyone in the household who should have been included, was included in the Census count.

It is also worth noting that some households and persons are included in the Census by proxy respondents. If a Census enumerator is unable to contact residents of a household after several attempts, the enumerators may seek data on the household from someone like a neighbor or a landlord. These are referred to as proxy respondents. People may be missed in the Census because proxy respondents are not aware of all the people who reside in a housing unit or may misidentify people by age.

In addition to unit nonresponse and item nonresponse, young children may not be reflected in the Census numbers because of processing errors in the Census operations, for example if the age imputation algorithm imputes an older age to a young child. In addition, there may appear to be a high net undercount of young children because the DA estimates are too high The potential errors in the DA estimates for young children was reviewed in Chap. 2, but there are a couple of additional thoughts explored here. For some of the ideas examined below, it is not clear whether the factor is more closely related to missed households or missed people within households.

7.2 Missing Households

In terms of thinking about ways to reduce the net undercount of young children in future Censuses, it would be extremely helpful to know what portion of the net undercount is due to young children living in households that were missed entirely compared to those missed because they were not included on a census question-naire that was returned. Unfortunately we do not have a good answer that question. But some of the information explored below may shed light on the issue.

As stated earlier, the results of the Census Bureau's Demographic Analysis shows a net undercount of 4.6 % or 970,000 people age 0–4 in the 2010 Census. But the Census Bureau's Census Coverage Measure (CCM) study (Census Bureau 2012a) found a net undercount of only 0.03 % of the 116,699,000 occupied hous-ing units (about 35,000).

If there was net undercount of only 35,000 occupied housing units but a net undercount of roughly 970,000 young children, it suggests that the high net under-count of young children is probably due to children being left off the Census forms that were returned by occupied households rather than children being missed because they were living in occupied housing units that were not captured in the Census. Alternatively, for the DA number of the net undercount of young children (970,000) and the CCM number on net undercount of occupied housing units (35,000) to be compatible, on average each missed occupied housing unit would have had about 28 children under age 5. This is not plausible.

The net undercount of 0.03 % of occupied housing units is comprised of roughly 1.9 % omissions and 1.9 % erroneous inclusions… 1.9 % of the total occupied housing units is 2.2 million housing units (U.S. Census Bureau 2012a). If 44 % of the omitted housing units had a young child and none of the errone-ously include housing units had a young children, it would account for the entire net undercount of young children. But the scenario that posits there were young children living in nearly half of missed housing units and none of the erroneously included housing units contained a young child is still unlikely.

There is similar data from the Census Bureau's American Community Survey. O'Hare and Jensen (2014) found that the coverage rate for the population age 0–4 in the 2009 American Community Survey (ACS) was only 89 % compared to 95 % for the adult population. But the household coverage rate in the 2009 American Community Survey as shown on the Census Bureau's website was 99 %. Again, if households are captured very well, but young children are not, it suggests that children are being left off questionnaires returned by households. It is reasonable to assume many of the same processes are operating in the Census and the ACS. Perhaps we can learn something about the undercount of young children in the Census by studying the yearly administration of the ACS.

Although the information above suggests the undercount of young children in the U.S. Census is due mostly to young children being left off Census questionnaires that are returned, Dolson (2013) found most of the young children that were missed in the 2011 Canadian Census were living in housing units that were missed, based on a reverse record check methodology. It is not clear how much weight to give this evidence because of differences in U.S. and the Canadian societies and difference in how the Censuses are undertaken and evaluated. In addition, the 2011 Canadian Census was somewhat unusual and controversial because it was made voluntary at the last minute.

7.2.1 Hard-to-Count Characteristics

In their examination of the net undercount of children, West and Robinson (1999, p. 7) conclude,

> The propensity for coverage errors for children may be exacerbated if the types of households, the types of living arrangements, and the types housing units we are most likely to miss in the Census include a disproportionate number of children.

There are several different aspects of this hypothesis that are explored here to see if they might help explain the high net undercount of young children relative to adults and older children.

There has been a stream of research at the Census Bureau since the 1990s aimed at identifying Hard-to-Count characteristics in the Census (Bruce et al. 2001; Bruce and Robinson 2003, 2007; Bruce et al. 2012). As part of its Planning Database the Census Bureau identified 12 characteristics that were used to construct Hard-to-Count scores for each Census tract in the 2000 Census. The Hard-to-Count characteristics are linked to low Mail Response/Return Rates and the likelihood of being missed in the Census.

Many of the variables identified as Hard-to-Count factors are also reflected in the model designed to identify characteristics of tracts with low Mail Return Rates (Erdman and Bates, 2014) as well as Hard-to-Count factors used in Great Britain (Abbott and Compton 2015).

The Hard-to-Count characteristics are used in two ways here. First, I look at the distribution of children in neighborhoods that are Hard-to-Count (identified here as those with low Mail Return Rates). Then I look at the concentration of children in households or living arrangements with Hard-to-Count characteristics.

7.2.2 Hard-to-Count Neighborhoods

While there are no undercount estimates at the Census tract level, Mail Return Rates are available for Census tracts and many experts believe that Mail Return Rates are closely related to net undercount rates. The Census Bureau Task Force on the Undercount of Young Children (Griffin 2014, p. ii) concluded, "Research suggests that areas with the lower levels of cooperation have higher levels of coverage and nonresponse error." Word (1997) notes, "...response rates and net undercount rates may be causally linked..." Also, recent work by Erdman and Bates (2014) implicitly link Mail Return Rates and net undercount rates. In describing the Low Response Score which is based on analysis of Mail Return Rates, the Census Bureau (2014a, p. 4) states, "This score identifies Block Groups and Tracts whose characteristics predict low Census Mail Return Rate and are highly correlated (negatively) with Census and survey participation."

It is important to recognize that the Mailout/Mailback operation is only the first part of the Census operations. Households that do not return a mailed Census questionnaire are visited by a Census Bureau enumerator. Nonetheless, the Mail Return Rate is often seen as an indicator of the likelihood of being missed in the Census.

I use the 2010 Mail Return Rates, to identify Census tracts that are Hart-to-Count. The Mail Return Rate is defined by the Census Bureau (2014a, p. 36) as:

> The number of mail returns received out of the total number of valid occupied housing units (HUs) in the Mailout/Mailback universe which excludes deleted, vacant, or units identified as undeliverable as addressed.

The 10 % of tracts with the lowest Mail Return Rates are classified as Hard-to-Count neighborhoods in the analysis below.

Data on the Census Mail Return Rates from the 2010 Census have recently been made available in the 2014 Census Planning Data Base (U.S. Census Bureau 2014a) which contains data for more than 73,000 Census tracts, including the number and percent of the population in each tract in various age groups. Data on young Blacks and Hispanics are not included in the Census Bureau's Planning Database, but I added 2010 Census data on Blacks and Hispanics by age to the file for the analysis shown in Table 7.1.

Table 7.1 shows the relative distribution of age groups in all Census tracts and the 10 % of Census Tracts that have the lowest Mail Return Rates. Data for Blacks and Hispanics by age are also shown in Table 7.1.

Young children are over-represented in the Hard-to-Count tracts (those with the lowest Mail Return Rates). The population age 0–4 comprises 8 % of the population in the tracts with the lowest Mail Return Rates, but only 6.5 % of the population in all tracts.

Interestingly, school-age children are not concentrated in the tracts with the lowest Mail Return Rates. The share of the population age 5–17 in all tracts (17.5 %) is almost identical to the share in the tracts with the lowest Mail Return Rates (17.6 %). The difference in the concentration in Hard-to-Count neighborhoods between preschool-age children and school-age children underscores the

importance of separating the 0–4-year-old population and the 5–17-year-old population in analysis of Census coverage.

Table 7.1 shows that Blacks and Hispanics of all ages are concentrated in the
Census tracts with the lowest Mail Return Rates, but young Blacks and Hispanics
are slightly more concentrated than other Black and Hispanic age groups. For the
Black Alone population of all ages, they are 13 % of the total population but 29 %
of the population in the Hard-to-Count tracts. Young Blacks (Alone) are slightly
more concentrated in Hard-to-Count tracts that all Blacks (Alone). The data are
somewhat similar for Hispanics but their concentration in Hard-to-Count Census
tracts is at a slightly lower level than for the Blacks Alone population. However,
Black and Hispanic school-age population are not any more concentrated in Hard-
to-Count neighborhoods than Blacks and Hispanics overall.

Table 7.1 Distribution of population by age and Race/Hispanic origin in all census tracts and
the 10 % of tracts with the lowest mail return rates

	All tracts		10 % of tracts with lowest mail return rates		Ratio of proportion in 10 % tracts to all tracts percent[a]
	Number (rounded to 1000 s)	Percent of total	Number (rounded to 1000 s)	Percent of total	
Population under age 5	20,193	7	2194	8	1.2
Population age 5–17	53,956	17	4851	18	1.0
Population age 18–24	30,641	10	4347	16	1.6
Population age 25–44	82,089	27	8077	29	1.1
Population age 45–64	81,449	26	5726	21	0.8
Population age 65+	40,247	13	2332	8	0.6
Black alone all ages	38,927	13	7884	29	2.3
Black alone age 0–4	2902	1	650	2	2.5
Black alone age 5–17	7938	3	1571	6	2.2
Hispanics all ages	50,468	16	8308	30	1.8
Hispanics age 0–4	5113	2	899	3	2.0
Hispanics age 5–17	12,014	4	1893	7	1.8
Total	308,574		27,527		

Source Authors analysis of data from U.S. Census Bureau (2014a, b)
[a]Ratios based on unrounded data

Based on the analysis of data in the 2014 Census Bureau's Planning Data Base, young children are 6.2 % of the population in Census tracts with poverty rates under 20 %, but they are 7.6 % of the population in Census tracts with poverty rates over 20 %, and 8.0 % of the population in Census tracts with poverty rates of 40 % or more. The school-age population (age 5–17) is not over-represented in high poverty tracts.

The results shown in Table 7.1 is consistent with other research. For example, the Annie E. Casey Foundation (2012) found only 4 % for Non-Hispanic White children under age 5 were living in high-poverty Census tracts while the rate for young Black children was 29 % and for young Hispanic children 20 %. To the extent that living in a high poverty Census tract reflects a Hard-to-Count environment, young minority children were living disproportionately in such places.

Moreover, data in Table 7.1 is related to several recent reports that have shown the concentration of poverty has surged since 2000 (U.S. Census Bureau 2014b; Jargowsky 2014; The Annie E. Casey Foundation 2012). The Census Bureau (2014b) indicates there was an increase of about 3 million children (age 0–17) living in poverty areas between 2000 and 2010. The analysis did not show data for children age 0–4 separately.

The high concentration of young Black and Hispanic children in Hard-to-Count areas and in high poverty neighborhoods is consistent with the high net undercount of young children in these groups. This finding is also consistent with the finding in Chap. 5 that a very high proportion of the net undercount of young children is accounted for in the in the largest counties in the country which probably reflects large cities in those counties and a disproportionate share of high poverty tracts and Hard-to-Count neighborhoods are located in large cities.

7.2.3 Hard-to-Count Characteristics

Hard-to-Count factors shown in Table 7.2 were derived by the Census Bureau to identify Census tracts that would be difficult to enumerate, but some of the factors can also be applied to individuals, families and households. Table 7.2 shows the percentages of young children (age 0–4), school-age children (age 5–17) and adults by ten Hard-to-Count characteristics identified by the Census Bureau (Bruce and Robinson 2003). Data for young Black and Hispanic children are also shown in Table 7.2.

Of the ten characteristics examined in Table 7.2, young children were more concentrated than adults in 8 of the 10 the Hard-to-Count categories. Adults were more concentrated in Other than Husband/Wife Households and slightly more concentrated in Buildings with 10 or More Units.

Table 7.2 shows young children were as concentrated or more concentrated than school-age children in all of the Hard-to-Count categories (for the percent of living in Other than a Husband/Wife Household they were the same) but the gap between younger and older children was often not as large as that seen between young children and adults.

Table 7.2 Distribution of population groups over ten hart-to-count characteristics from the census bureau's planning data base

	Percent of adults in this kind of situation	Percent of children age 5–17 in this kind of situation	Percent of children age 0–4 in this kind of situation		
			Total	Black	Hispanic
Population living in building with 10+ units	10	6	9	16	15
Population living in building with 2+ units	20	16	24	43	35
Population living in rental unit	30	35	45	70	60
Population living in crowded households (more than one person per room)	6	13	17	19	35
Population living in something other than husband/wife household	41	34	34	67	40
Population in housing units with no phone	2	2	3	4	3
Population living below the poverty level	16	21	26	46	36
Percent living in housing receiving food stamps[a]	15	22	29	54	37
Population living in linguistically isolated households	5	6	8	3	25
Population who moved between 2009 and 2010[b]	15	14	21	27	23

Source Authors analysis of 2010 ACS PUMS on the IPUMS system at the University of Minnesota
[a]Planning Data Base uses Public Assistance Income instead of Food Stamps
[b]Data for young children reflect ages 1–4

   Data in Table 7.2 also show young Black or Hispanic children are highly concentrated in Hard-to-Count categories. In every case, young Black and Hispanic children were more concentrated in the Hard-to-Count categories than adults or older children. In many cases, the percentages for young Black or Hispanic children in the Hard-to-Count categories are two or three times those of adults.

Data in Tables 7.1 and 7.2 suggests that one reason young children have high net undercount rates is related to the fact they are more concentrated than adults or older children in the kinds of neighborhoods, households and living arrangements that are linked to being missed in the Census.

7.2.4 Race, Hispanic Origin and Immigrant Status

Historically, Blacks, Hispanics and American Indians have had above average Census net undercount rates (Edmonston 2002; West and Robinson 1999; Schwede et al. 2015). Analysis shown earlier in this paper indicate young Black Alone or in Combination children and young Hispanic children have net undercount rates that were more than twice as high as their Non-Black or Non-Hispanic counterparts (see Table 3.1). Schwede et al. (2015, Table 14.1) show American Indians living on reservations had high net undercount rates in the 1990 and 2010 Censuses. The fact that the net undercount rates are high for adults as well as children for these groups suggests that the problem is more likely due to omitted households rather than people omitted within households.

Asian Americans were not included in this group because the data regarding undercounts for this group are not clear. Only the CCM method provides estimates for the 2010 Census coverage of Asian. The CCM estimates for Asians are close to zero and the standard errors indicate the estimates for the undercounts of this group are not statistically significantly different from zero. Given the diversity in the Asian America population, is it likely that subgroups of Asians have very different census coverage experiences.

Table 7.3 shows Blacks, Hispanics and American Indians are a disproportionately large share of young children. Table 7.3 shows Black, Hispanic and American Indian/Alaskan Natives are 41 % of the population age 0–4, but only 33 % of the population age 15–17. They are 28 % of the adult population. To the extent that racial/Hispanic minorities comprise a disproportionately large share of the young child population it may help explain the higher net undercount rate of young children.

Although there are no direct measures of the undercount of immigrants, many people believe this population is among the most difficult to enumerate (Kissam

Table 7.3 Percent age 0–4, age 15–17, and age 18 and older who are black alone, Hispanic, or American Indian/Alaskan native alone: 2010

	Percent black alone or Hispanic, or American Indian/Alaskana native alone
Age 0–4	41
Age 15–17	33
Age 18 or older	28

Source U.S. Census Bureau, 2010 Census, Summary File 1, Tables P12H, P12B, P12C, and QT-P1

and Jacobs 1999). If young children are over-represented in immigrant households, it could help explain the high net undercount for this population. However, Table 7.4 shows that young children are about as concentrated in immigrant families as older children. About a quarter of each age group in the 0–17 age range are living immigrant families, defined here as a family where one or more parent(s) is foreign-born. So it does not appear that the higher net undercount rate for young children compared to older children is related to differences in the percent living in immigrant families.

There are no solid statistical data on this issue, but some people believe there are difficulties counting undocumented immigrants in the Census (Massey 2015; Branche, no date) and there is some evidence that children are a significant part of the undocumented population and/or are living in households with undocumented individuals. A recent report (Passel et al. 2014a) found that there were about one million unauthorized immigrants who are children (under age 18). In addition Taylor et al. (2011) found 4.5 million children (people under age 18) were born in the United States to at least one unauthorized immigrant parent. Yoshikawa et al. (2014) found that 5.5 million children (age 0–17) currently reside with at least one undocumented immigrant parent. It would be useful to know if young children are over-represented in undocumented population or in households with undocumented residents. However, according to data on the website of the Migration Policy Institute, only 76,000 of the 11.4 million undocumented immigrants are less than age 5 so problems counting undocumented immigrants in the U.S. Census would not have much impact on young children.

While young children living in households with undocumented residents may be at risk of being undercounted at a high rate, the net undercount rate for young Hispanic children (7.5 %) is only slightly higher than that for Black Alone or in Combination children (6.3 %). If families with unauthorized members were a driving force in the high net undercount rate of young children, one would expect it to affect Hispanic disproportionately since almost 80 % of the undocumented population are from Latin America (Passel et al. 2014b, p. 18).

Table 7.4 Percent of child population living in immigrant families by age: 2012

Age	Percent of children in immigrant families[a]
0	26
1 and 2	26
3–5	26
6–8	27
9–11	25
12–14	24
15–17	24

Source U.S. Federal Interagency Forum on Child and Families Statistics (2013) Table FAM4

[a]Immigrant families are those where one or both parents are foreign-born

7.2.5 *Young Children and Respondent Barriers*

It is possible that having young children in the household inhibits responses to the Census questionnaire. Examination of survey data taken prior to and during the 2010 Census enumeration phase shows that having more than two children in the household lowers the likelihood of respondents saying they will participate in the 2010 Census independent of other factors (Walejko et al. 2011). Keep in mind that this analysis only relates to stated intention to participate not actual participation and participation of the adult does not necessarily mean that children in the household will be included on the Census questionnaire. The study did not examine the impact of young children (under age 5) separately from all children.

With regard to completing the Census questionnaire, Hillygus and colleagues (2006, p. 103) note,

> Respondents who are married with children have a lower mail-back rate (83 %) than those who are married without children (90 %), suggesting that the time demands of child care work against taking on this particular duty.

Another aspect of the data presented by Hillygus and colleagues also supports this idea. Hillygus and colleagues (2006, Table 4.4) show only 63 % of single parents mailed back their Census questionnaire in 2000. Presumably single parents must devote a larger share of their time to child care than married-couple families. Unfortunately, Hillygus and colleagues did not look at the impact of young children (under age 5) separately from all children.

To the extent that child care responsibilities dampen Census response rates, there is clear evidence that young children require more parental time and attention than older children. A report from the U.S. Bureau of Labor Statistics (2011, p. 3) regarding time use in 2010, concluded,

> Adults living in households with children under 6 spent an average of 2.0 h per day providing childcare to household children. Adults living in households where the youngest child was between the ages of 6 and 17 spent less than half as much time providing primary child care to household children.

For families with many children and/or young children demands of child care may decrease Census participation.

The Census Bureau's analysis of Mail Return Rates in the 2010 Census did not include examination of households by marital status and/or presence or age of children in the household (Letourneau 2012). One piece of data from the 2010 analysis that seems relevant to the effect of child care demands on Census participation is the Mail Return Rate by size of household which shows that larger households have lower Mail Return Rates. Data from 2010 show that 84 % of 2-person households mailed back their Census questionnaire compared to 72 % of 7-person households. Larger household are more likely to have young children. Perhaps the data on mail-back rates in the 2010 Census could be re-examined to see if they are consistent with those from 2000 with respect to marital status and the presence of children. If such re-analysis is undertaken, it would be useful to examine the mail-back rates by the presence of young children.

Time pressures of child care may also result in respondent fatigue. Beimer et al. (1991, p. 40) state, "...if the interview is long, fatigue, both for the respondent and the interviewers, may be a factor in reducing the willingness to respond fully ..."

In that context, it is noteworthy that young children are about three times as likely as adults to live in a large household. The ACS data from 2010 indicate 10.1 % of young children live in large households (more than 6 people) compared to 3.5 % of adults. Consequently, filling out the Census questionnaire for those households takes more time and may lead to respondent fatigue.

It is also important to note that respondents typically fill in the Census questionnaire from the oldest to the youngest person. Wetrogan and Crease (2001, p. iii) conclude that "...children are generally listed after adults on questionnaires filled out by respondents." Griffin (2014, Table 4) indicates that the population age 0–4 is only 6.5 % of the population, but accounts for 30.3 % of the persons in person number slot 7 and higher on the Census questionnaire. The person number slot indicates the order in which people are entered onto the Census questionnaire. Hill (2011) shows children are more likely to be listed after adults in the 2010 Census.

Any problem with completing the Census questionnaire or following-up with large households would affect young children disproportionately for two reasons. Young children are more likely than adults to live in large households and young children are usually entered last on the Census Questionnaire.

7.3 Children Omitted on Census Questionnaires that Are Returned

In addition to young children who are not counted because their whole household was missed, some young children may be missed because they were left off Census questionnaires that were returned. Children may be omitted because they are left off a questionnaire that was mailed back, missed by an interviewer or enumerator during the Non-Response Followup procedure, or possibly missed in another way such as an incorrect proxy response.

Some children are left off Census questionnaires inadvertently, in part, because respondents may not understand the residence rules of the Census. Other children may be left off Census questionnaires on purpose, either because respondents think the Census is not interested in information on children or because the respondent wants to conceal a young child from the authorities. Despite assurances from the Census Bureau about the confidentiality of responses to the Census, many people believe that data given to the Census Bureau may be shared with other government agencies.

7.3.1 Changing Family Structure and Living Arrangements

Some children are left off Census questionnaires because respondents are unsure of their status within the household. The uncertainty about whether or not to include a young child as a household resident is probably higher for complex and non-traditional households. In response to changes in family structure and living arrangements, the Census Bureau Task Force on the Undercount of Young Children (Griffin 2014, p. II) concluded, "In particular, research that will document, profile and target the growing number of 'complex households' can set a strong foundation for new methods to improve their enumeration."

According to West and Robinson (1999, p. 10),

> The Census rules of residence instruct that the person in whose name the house or apartment is owned, being bought or rented be listed as person 1 on the form. The respondent is then asked to identify members of the household in relation to person 1. This often contradicts the respondent's notion of family or household.

The "usual place of residence" is a key concept used by the in the Census, but Martin (1999, 2007) argues that concept is not always clear to respondents and attachment to a single household may be more of a continuous concept rather than a dichotomous one. Moreover, most of the rules respondents use to determine who they think lives in their household (economic contributions, doing household chores, receiving mail at the address) do not apply to young children (Martin 2007).

West and Robinson (1999, p. 9) conclude one situation that may lead to a child being missed in the Census is,

> A child who resides in a diverse household structure and in a unique living arrangement among multiple nuclear families…Unusual living arrangements involving children that make it difficult for the respondent to roster the household correctly on the Census form, e.g. presence of multiple nuclear families, unrelated children or stepchildren of the respondent.

Several recent studies have underscored changes in family structure and living arrangements in the U.S. that may impact census coverage for children. For example Kochhar and Cohn (2011) found the economic downturn just prior to the 2020 Census "helped fuel the largest increase in the number of Americans living in multi-generational households in modern history." Of the 51.4 million people in multi-generation households, 9.6 are children age 0–17. Mykata and Macartney (2012) show that the number of shared households (defined as a household with at least one resident adult who is not enrolled in school and who is neither the householder nor spouse or cohabiting partner of the householder) went from 12.5 million in 2007 to 14.7 million in 2010. In a recent report based on Census Bureau data Livingston (2014, p. 1) stated, "Less than half (46 %) of U.S. kids younger than 18 years of age are living in a home with two married heterosexual parents in their first marriage." In 1960, 73 % of children were living in the type of traditional households described above. Are children age 0–4 over-represented in these types of families? Like the other two articles cited in the paragraph above, Livingston did not break out the data by age so we could see if the situation for young children was different that the situation for older children.

If young children are over-represented in complex or non-traditional households it may help explain the high net undercount of young children. The information below sheds some light on this topic.

Table 7.5 shows how young children compare to adults and school-age children on three measures reflecting complex living arrangements. In every case young children, and particularly young minority children, are more concentrated than older children or adults in kinds of non-traditional or complex households examined.

The data in Table 7.5 is consistent with Pilkauskis (2012) who found a greater presence of very young children in 3-generational families compared to older children. She interviewed parents living in 3-generational families, identified by sampling birth records, and oversampling non-married couples. She found the proportion of children living in multi-generation households declined by age of child from 17.6 % at birth to only 7.6 % by age 9. The 2010 ACS shows that almost half (48 %) of children under age 18 living with grandparents were under age 5.

Table 7.5 Selected living arrangements of adults and children by age and Race/Hispanic origin in 2010

	Percent of adults in this kind of situation	Percent of all children in this kind of situation	Percent of children age 5–17 in this kind of situation	Percent of children age 0–4 in this kind of situation		
				Total	Black	Hispanic
Percent of population living in 3+ generation households	7	11	10	13	21	19
Percent of population living a household with one or more subfamilies	6	9	8	14	20	20
Percent of Population in households with more than one family	14	11	10	15	15	22

Source Authors analysis of 2010 American Community Survey Public-Use Microdata file analyzed on IPUMS system at the University of Minnesota

One official at the Census Bureau "…noted that she was aware of instances with multiple families, for example, where the household respondent did not include children in the second family." (Cited in Griffin 2014, p. 16). The presence of subfamilies in a household could make correct rostering of household members more complicated.

Figure 7.1 shows that younger children are more likely than older children to be living in a subfamily. Almost 13 % of children under one year of age are living in a subfamily compared to only 5 % of those age 15–17.

The most rapidly growing type of living arrangement for children (percentage-wise) is in cohabitating households. The number of children living in cohabiting households (presence of an unmarried partner of the householder) climbed from 4.4 million in 2005 to 5.5 million in 2010 (author downloaded ACS data from American Factfinder). Census Bureau reports that there was an unusually large increase in cohabiting couples between 2009 and 2010 (Krieder 2010).

Since cohabiting couples reflect living arrangements that are relatively unstable (compared to married-couple families) and the relationships among adults and children are different from those in a nuclear family, it would not be surprising if a disproportionately high share of children in these types of living arrangements were not being reported in the Census. Data from the Census Bureau's Survey of Income and Program Participation (U.S. Census Bureau 2011) indicate 10 % of children age 0–4 are were living in cohabitating households compared to 6 % of children age 5–14.

Newborns may be particularly likely to be living in a complex households A recent report from the Census Bureau (Monte and Ellis 2014, p. 2) found "more than one in five women with a birth in the past 12 months reported at the time of the survey that they were living in someone else's home." In another analysis (Gooding 2008) shows that 13 % of mothers are not co-residing with their biological child under age 1 and rates are higher for Blacks and Hispanics where the net undercount of children is also higher.

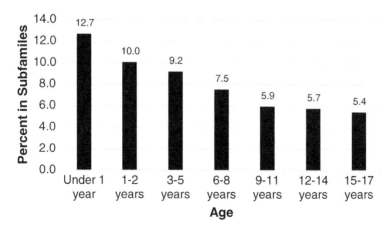

Fig. 7.1   Percent of children in subfamilies by age: 2014. *Source* U.S. Census Bureau (2015)

Schwede and Terry (2013, p. 89) concluded, "Additionally, the situation of mobility of children cycling between housing units and trying to determine from time spent in each where they should be counted was a reason for inconsistencies."

To the extent that changes in family transitions may lead to uncertainty about where to count an individual in the Census, young children experience more transitions than older children. A recent report from the Census Bureau (Laughlin 2014) shows that 31 % of children age 0–5 had a family structure transition (change in the number of parents or parent's partners) between 2008 and 2011 compared to only 13 % of children age 6–17 year old.

Martin (1999, 2007) shows that being related to the household respondent in a survey greatly decreases ambiguity related to residential attachment. But some evidence suggests that being related to the householder does not diminish net undercount rates for children. Younger children are more likely than older children to be related to the householder The 2010 ACS shows about 1.5 % of young children age 0–4 were not related to the householder compared to 4.2 % of 14-to-17-year-olds. But as shown earlier in this paper, younger children have higher net undercount rates than older children. On the other hand, Black Alone and Hispanic young children have above average net undercount rates, and they are also slightly less likely than Non-Hispanic White children to be related to householders. Based on the 2010 ACS, about 2 % of Black Alone and 2 % of Hispanic children age 0–4 are not related to the householder, compared to 1.3 % of Non-Hispanic Whites.

In the context of being related to the householder, data from the Census Bureau's Survey of Income and Program Participation indicate 3 % of children age 0–4 were living with neither parent compared to 4 % of children age 5–14. One situation when a child is living with neither parent is in foster care. In recent years there have typically been about 400,000 children in foster care at any point in time, and for many of these children their usual place of resident may not be clear. Young children are over-represented in this population. About 38 % of children in foster care are under age 5. O'Hare (2008) shows that about half of the children in foster care are grandchildren living with grandparents in kinship care so they are probably included in the Census as grandchildren of the householder and the other half are captured in the Census at a pretty high rate.

7.3.2 Questionnaire Design

The design of the Census questionnaire may contribute to net undercount of young children. In discussing possible reasons for the high net undercount of children in the Census, writing just prior to the 2000 Census West and Robinson (1999) state one reason may be, "Limitations of the Census questionnaire that make it difficult for the respondent to include all children, who are likely to be listed last, e.g. lack of space on the form if the household has many members."

In discussing the net undercount of children, West and Robinson (1999, p. 6) also conclude, "Coverage errors are likely to occur because the respondent has difficulty rostering his or her household." This is more likely to happen in complex households.

A recent paper by Battle and Bielick (2014) also suggest that the inclusion of young children may be particularly sensitive to the way rostering is done. Battle and Bielick found that when a full household screener is used (similar to the Census questionnaire) young children are under-represented relative to using a child screener.

On the Mailout/Mailback Census questionnaire that was used in the 2010 Census there is only room for complete demographic information for six people in the household. There is limited room for the names and a few characteristics for persons 7 through 12. If more than 12 people lived in the household, the Census Bureau had to follow up to get complete information for these people. Any difficulties collecting data for children in the largest households (13 or more people) are not likely to be major problem because so few children live in such households.

On the form used for Non-Response Followup (NRFU) in the 2010 Census, there is only room for data on five people on the primary form. However, the fact that the NRFU form is used by trained enumerators, often collecting the data in person, should mitigate this shortcoming in the form.

The limited number of spaces for full information for individuals on the Census form would only be a potential problem for large households, i.e. those with more than 6 people (West and Robinson 1999). As noted earlier, the ACS data from 2010 indicate 10.1 % of young children live in large households (more than 6 people) compared to 3.5 % of adults.

It is important to note that some potential problems with the structure of the Census questionnaire were more likely to have been a problem with the 2000 and 1990 questionnaire rather than the 2010 questionnaire. Numerous improvements were made to the Census Mailout/Mailback questionnaire between 2000 and 2010 to eliminate or minimize previous problems (O'Hare 2009). Perhaps the most notable improvement is that the main Census questionnaire used in the 2010 Census asks for the age of persons in the Census questionnaire slots number 7 through 12. So unlike in the 1990 and 2000 Censuses, even if no follow up occurs, the Census Bureau has the age of everyone in the household who is listed.

The impact of improvements in the Census questionnaire between 2000 and 2010 is unclear. There were improvements in the Census questionnaire between 2000 and 2010, but the net undercount of young children increased slightly between 2000 and 2010 from 3.8 to 4.6 %. On the other hand, some of the new instructions on the 2010 Census questionnaire were aimed specifically at infants and newborns, and there does seem to be an improvement in the coverage for age 0 between the 2000 and the 2010 Census as shown in Chap. 3.

7.3.3 Children Deliberately Concealed

There is some evidence to support the idea that some children may purposively be left off returned Census questionnaires. Either because respondents don't think the Census Bureau wants information on young children or because respondents don't want the Census Bureau (or any government agency) to know about the child.

A series of short surveys by the Census Bureau (Nichols et al. 2014a, b, c) respondents were asked, "What information do you think the Census typically collects every 10 years?" and were offered several choices. The percentage who thought the Census Bureau collects "Names of children living at your address" was 7–9 % points lower than the percentage who thought the Census Bureau collects, "Names of adults living at your address." While this question asks about names rather than about information on individuals, it suggests that some people think the Census does not request information on children. It would be useful to know if respondents would make a distinction between young children and older children in the question above.

In their qualitative study of 2010 Census respondents Schwede and Terry (2013) indicated many respondents do not believe the Census Bureau (or the federal government) wants young children included in the Census count. Note this is for all children not just young children. It would be useful to see if there was a difference in responses for children age 0–4 and those age 5–17.

The report of the Census Bureau Task Force on the Undercount of Young Children (Griffin 2014, p. 16) states one of the reasons children are left off forms is, "Respondents deliberately not mentioning kids for fear of some reprisals or bad outcomes from landlords, immigration agencies, social service agencies, etc." In their discussion of the undercount of children, West and Robinson (1999, p. 7) also conclude,

> Listing some members of the households may have other negative consequences. For example, a respondent may fear that disclosure of certain members of the household will affect eligibility for social services, that children illegally in the country will be deported., or that the whereabouts of a child in hiding from a custodial parent will be detected.

Pitkin and Park (2005) also mention "systematic concealment" as a potential reason children are undercounted in the Census. To the extent that respondents feel older children may already be "in the system" because they are in school, concealment may impact younger children at a higher rate. It would be useful to know if parental efforts to conceal children in the Census affects younger children more than older children. Ethnographic research might shed light on this issue.

7.4 Estimation Errors

Recall that the net undercount figures are a product of omissions and erroneous enumerations (mostly people included twice). For example, the 0.1 % net overcount for the total population in the 2010 Census was the product of 9.9 million erroneous enumerations, 6 million whole person imputations, and 15 million omissions (U.S. Census Bureau 2012b, Table 2).

It is possible that the high net undercount of young children is partially a product of low double counting or erroneous enumerations for this group rather than a high omission rate. The only data about overcounts and undercounts for the 2010 Census come from Census Coverage Measurement (CCM). While the CCM data

Table 7.6 Duplicates in the 2010 census by age

Age in years	Duplicates found		All persons enumerated	
	In the census		In the census	
	Number (in 1000 s)	Percent	Number (in 1000 s)	Percent
Under 5 years	448	6	20,201	6.5
5–9 years	526	7.1	20,349	6.6
10–14 years	581	7.8	20,677	6.7
15–19 years	854	11.5	22,040	7.1
20 years +	4862	65.3	225,478	73
Inconsistent	171	2.4	NA	NA
Missing	12	0.2	NA	NA
Total	7454	100	308,746	100

Source U.S. Census Bureau, Heimel and King (2012)

on undercounts of young children are suspect with respect to the overall net under-count of young children because of correlation bias, as discussed in Chap. 2, it is one of the few pieces of information we have to address this question.

Census Burau data indicate that the level of duplication for persons age 0–4 is very similar to those age 5–9, and 10–17. Based on the CCM results, the percent of the population age 0–4 that were duplicated in 2010 was 3.2 %, compared to 3.0 for age 5–9 and 3.2 for age 10–17. It is also noteworthy that the omission rate for young children (6.6 %) is substantially higher than those for age 5–9 (4.9 %) and age 10–17 (4.4 %). The data does not support the idea that there is a high net undercount of young children because there was a high duplication rate.

There is another piece of information from the 2010 Census that is related to the duplication of young children. While conducting the 2010 Census the Census Bureau used a sophisticated computer-matching algorithm to try and find and eliminate duplication of responses (Heimel and King 2012). If there were too many duplicates erroneously included in the 2010 Census count, it would mean the Census count was too high and the net undercount of young children was actu-ally higher than the 4.6 % observed.

Table 7.6 shows that children age 0–4 were 6.5 % of enumerated population but only 6.0 % of the duplicates found. In other words, young children were only slightly under-represented in the duplicates that were found.

7.4.1 Potential Census Processing Errors

When people fail to provide a valid age on the Census questionnaire, the Census Bureau must impute, substitute, or allocate a figure. This is done largely based on known characteristics of the household or the neighborhood using a "hot deck" method. If the Census Bureau imputed, substituted, or allocated too few young

Table 7.7 Distribution of population by age before and after allocation

	NOT allocated		Allocated		Sum of allocated and not allocated	
	Number (in 1000 s)	Percent	Number (in 1000 s)	Percent	Number (in 1000 s)	Percent
0–4	19,224	6.6	543	5.1	19,767	6.5
5–13	35,203	12.1	934	8.7	36,137	11.9
14–17	16,379	5.6	422	3.9	16,801	5.6
18+	221,136	75.7	8839	82.3	229,975	76
Total	291,943	100	10,739	100	302,682	100

Source Derived from Griffin (2014, Table 4)

children into the Census count that would partially explain the high net undercount of young children.

However, only 3.6 % of people (of all ages) had their age imputed in the 2010 Census (U.S. Census Bureau 2011) so it seems unlikely that misassignment of age would be major factor in the net undercount of the 0–4 population.

Table 7.7 shows the population age 0–4 had age allocated at a slightly lower percent than one would expect based on their percentage of the unallocated population. This was true of all ages under age 18. The 0–4 population was 6.6 % of the population that did not have their age allocated, but only 5.1 % of the population with age allocated.

It is possible that age misallocation may explain a small part of the high net undercount for young children, but it appears that age misallocation is not likely to be a major source of the high net undercount for young children. The Census Bureau's Task Force on the Undercount of Young Children (Griffin 2014, p. 8) concludes "These findings showed no evidence that the hot deck systematically allocated ages other than 0–4 thus contributing to an undercount."

7.4.2 Potential Errors in DA Estimation

If the DA estimates were too high, it would result in an upward bias in the net undercount estimates. Potential errors in the DA estimates were reviewed in Chap. 2, but there is one more idea explored here.

Pitkin and Park (2005) show that the expected number of children age 0–4 of foreign-born mothers in California based on birth certificate data is 13 % higher than an estimate based on 2000 Census data. Pitkin and Park (2005, p. 10) conclude, "…it is possible and perhaps not unreasonable to speculate that the 'missed' children of foreign-bon White and API mothers in California have emigrated." Pitkin and Park (2005, p. 5) hypothesize that "…children who were born in California had left the U.S. before the Census and had emigrated i.e. there was not an undercount and the A.C.E. was right."

In this context, it is also noteworthy that almost all of the counties along the U.S./Mexico border, which is probably the geographic area where one would expect to see the phenomenon described by Pitkin and Part most often, have higher net undercounts of young children (O'Hare 2013). Of course, these counties typically have many Hart-to-Count characteristics as well.

As far as I can tell, other researchers have not pursued this argument, perhaps, in part, because there are a couple aspects of the study that are worrisome. Since Pitkin and Park used the 1 % PUMS file to estimates the number of children born to foreign-born mothers in California and they were forced to make several tenuous assumptions about household and family relationships in the PUMS file to identify children of foreign-born mothers born in California. Also the 1 % PUMS file which has significant sampling error for small groups.

Although the analysis by Pitkin and Park is focused on California, nationally the net undercount rate for Hispanics age 0–4 in 2000 was 7.7 % but the net overcount rate for Hispanic age 10–14 in 2010 was 1.9 %. If the net undercount rates of Hispanics age 0–4 in 2000 was due to undetected emigration, one would not expect there to be an overcount of the same age cohort in 2010 when they were age 10–14.

It is possible that undetected emigration of young children born in the U.S. may explain a portion of the net undercount of young children, but it is difficult for me to believe that it could account for a very large share of the 970,000 net undercount of young children seen in the 2010 Census.

7.5 Summary

Several potential explanations for the high net undercount of young children were examined and statistical data or other evidence, to the extent it exists, were provided for each potential explanation. While there is more support for some potential explanations that for other, none seem compelling.

- The evidence reviewed here suggests that the net undercount of young children is more likely due to young children being left off Census questionnaires that are returned rather than being missed because the household where they live was not included in the census. But this still largely an open question.
- There is strong evidence that young children are a disproportionately high share of people living in the kinds of neighborhoods, families, and living arrangements where the population is difficult to enumerate. Young Black and Hispanic children are particularly concentrated in Hard-to-Count situations.
- Young children may be missed because they are more likely to live in complex or non-traditional households where their status in the household is unclear.
- Hispanics, Blacks and American Indians/Alaskan Natives are a disproportionately large share of young children compared to older children and adults and these groups have high net undercount rates.

- Young children are not more concentrated in immigrant families than older children.
- The child care burdens of young children may contribute to the net undercount of young children, but the evidence is circumstantial and weak.
- Young children may be missed because respondents want to conceal them from the government, in part, because of fear or reprisals or negative outcomes.
- The design of the Census questionnaire may contribute to the high net undercount of young children because young children are a disproportionately high share of those living in large households and young children are typically listed last on the Census questionnaire.
- There is no strong evidence that young children are under-imputed by the Census algorithm.

Perhaps the most fundamental conclusion from the material reviewed in this Chapter is that there is very little solid information in the literature regarding reasons for the high net undercount of young children. And the information that is available is not very compelling. Clearly, more research is needed on the reasons for the high net undercount of young children.

References

Abbott, O., & Compton, G. (2015). Counting and estimating hard-to-survey populations. In R. Tourangeau, B. Edwards, T. P. Johnson, K. M. Wolter, & N. Bates (Eds.), *Hard-to-survey populations* (pp. 37–57). Cambridge: Cambridge University Press.

Battle, D., & Bielick, S. (2014, June). *Differences in coverage and nonresponse when using a full household enumeration screener versus a child-only screener in a 2013 national mail survey*. Paper presented at Annual Conference of the American Association of Public Opinion Research, Anaheim, CA.

Beimer, P. P., Groves, R. M., Lyberg, L. E., Mathiowetz, N. A., & Sudman, S. (1991) *Measurement errors in surveys*. New York: Wiley.

Branche, A. (no date). *The next economic imperative: Undocumented immigrants in the 2010 census*. Drum Major Institute for Public Policy,

Bruce, A., & Robinson, J. G. (2003, Oct 24). *The planning database: Its development and use as an effective tool in census 2000*. Paper presented at the Annual Meeting of the Southern Demographic Association, Arlington, VA.

Bruce, A., & Robinson, J. G. (2007). *Tract level planning database with census 2000 data*. Washington, DC: U.S. Census Bureau.

Bruce, A., Robinson, J. G., Devine, J. E. (2012). A planning database to identify areas that are hard-to-enumerate and hard to survey in the United States. In *Proceedings of the International Conference on Methods for Surveying and Enumerating Hard-to-Reach Populations*. American Statistical Association.

Bruce, A., Robinson, J. G., & Sanders, M. V. (2001). Hard-to-count scores and broad demographic groups associated with patterns of response rates in census 2000. In *Proceedings of the Social Statistics Section*. American Statistical Association.

de la Puente, M. (1993). *Using ethnography to explain why people are missed or erroneously included by the census: evidence from small area ethnographic research*. U.S. Census Bureau.

Dolson, D. (2013). *Differential coverage error for young children in the Canadian census*. Presentation at the Joint Statistical Meeting, Montreal, Canada August.

Edmonston, B. (2002). *The undercount in the 2000 census.* A KIDS COUNT/PRB Report on Decennial Census 2000, The Annie E. Casey Foundation, Baltimore, MD. T.

Erdman, C., & Bates, N. (2014). *The census bureau mail return rate challenge: Crowdsourcing to development hard-to-count scores.* Washington, DC: U.S. Census Bureau.

Gooding, G. E. (2008, August). *Differences between coresident and non-coresident women with a recent birth.* Annual Meeting of the American Sociological Society, Boston, MA.

Griffin, D. H. (2014, 2 February) *Final task force report: Task force on the undercount of young children.* Memorandum for Frank A. Vitrano, U.S. Census Bureau, Washington, DC.

Heimel, S., & King, R. (2012). *2010 census effectiveness of unduplication evaluation report.* 2010 Census Planning Memoranda Series #244.

Hill, J. M. (2011). *Estimated percent of children listed by person box on the 2010 decennial census mailout/mailback questionnaire.* DSSD 2010 Decennial Census Memorandum Series #G-37. U.S. Census Bureau, Washington, DC.

Hillygus, S. D., Nie, N. H., Prewitt, K., & Pals, H. (2006). *The hard count: The political and social challenges of census mobilization.* New York: Russell Sage Foundation.

Jargowsky, P. A. (2014). Concentration of poverty in the new millennium. *Changes in prevalence, composition and location of high poverty neighborhoods.* A report by the Century Foundation and Rutgers Center for Urban Research and Education.

Kassim, E., & Jacobs, I. J. (1999, September). *Census undercount and immigration integration into rural California life.* Davis: University of California.

Kochhar, R., & Cohn, D. (2011, October). *Fighting poverty in a bad economy: American's move in with relatives.* Washington DC: Pew Research Center.

Laughlin, L. (2014). *A child's day: Living arrangements, nativity and family transitions: 2011 (Selected Indicators of Child Well-Being).* Current Population Reports, P70-139, The U.S. Census Bureau, Washington DC.

Letourneau, E. (2012). *Mail response/return rates assessment.* 2010 Census Planning Memorandum Series, No. 198, U.S. Census Bureau, Washington DC.

Livingston, G. (2014*). Less than half of U.S. kids today live in a 'traditional' family.* Washington, DC: Pew Research Center.

Martin, E. (1999). Who knows who lives here? Within-household disagreements as a source of survey coverage error. *Public Opinion Quarterly, 63,* 220–236.

Martin, E. (2007). Strength of attachment: Survey coverage of people with tenuous ties to residences. *Demography, 44*(2), 437–440.

Martin, E., & de la Puente, M. (1993). *Research on sources of undercoverage within households.* Washington, DC: U.S. Census Bureau.

Massey, D. S. (2015). Challenges to surveying immigrants. In R. Tourangeau, B. Edwards, T. P. Johnson, K. M. Wolter, & N. Bates (Eds.), *Hart-to-survey populations* (pp. 270–292). Cambridge: Cambridge University Press.

Monte, L. M., & Ellis, R. R. (2014). *Fertility of women in the United States: 2012.* Current Population Reports, P20-75, U.S. Bureau of the Census, Washington, DC.

Mykata, L., & Macartney, S. (2012, June). Sharing a household: Household composition and economic well-being: 2007–2010. U.S. Census Bureau, Current Population Reports, P60-242.

Nichols, E., King, R., & Childs, J. (2014a, March 27). *Small-scale testing pilot test results: Testing email and address collection screens and Census opinion questions using a nonprobability panel.* Internal memorandum to Burton Reist, Census Bureau.

Nichols, E., King, R., and Childs, J. (2014b, May 27). *2014 March Small-Scale Testing Pilot Test Results: Testing email subject lines, email formats, address collection screens and Census opinion questions using a nonprobability panel.* Internal memorandum to Burton Reist, Census Bureau.

Nichols, E., King, R., & Childs, J. (2014c, September 9). *May 2104 small-scale testing results: Testing email subject lines, email formats, address collection screens and Census opinion questions using a nonprobability panel.* Internal memorandum to Burton Reist, U.S. Census Bureau.

O'Hare, W. P. (2008). *Data on children in foster care from the census bureau.* Baltimore, MD: The Annie E. Casey Foundation.

O'Hare, W. P. (2009). *Why are young children missed so often in the census.* KIDS COUNT Working Paper, December, The Annie E. Casey Foundation, Baltimore, MD.

O'Hare, W. P. (2013). *Difference between 2010 census counts and vintage 2010 population estimates for age 0–4 at the state and county level.* Poster presented at the 2013 Annual Conference of the Population Association of America, New Orleans, LA.

O'Hare, W. P., & Jensen, E. B. (2014, May 29–30). *The representation of young children in the American community survey.* Presentation at the ACS Users Group Conference, Washington, DC.

Olson, D. B. (2009). A three-phase model of census capture. Paper presented at the Joint Statistical Meetings.

Passel, J. S., Lopez, M. H., Cohn, D., & Rohal, M. (2014a). *As growth stalls, unauthorized immigrant population becomes more settled.* Washington, DC: Pew Research Center, Pew Hispanic Center.

Passel, J. S., Cohn, D., & Rohal, M. (2014b). *Unauthorized immigrant totals rise in 7 states, fall in 14.* Washington, DC: Pew Research Center, Pew Hispanic Center.

Pilkauskas, N. V. (2012). Three-generation family households: Differences by family structure at birth. *Journal of Marriage and Family 74,* 931–943.

Pitkin, J., & Park, J. (2005, March). *The gap between births and census counts of children born in California: Undercount or transnational movement?* Paper presented at the Population Association of America Conference, Philadelphia PA.

Schwede, L., & Terry, R. (2013). *Comparative ethnographic studies of enumeration methods and coverage across race and ethnic groups.* 2010 Census Program for Evaluations and Experiments, U.S. Census Bureau, Washington, DC.

Schwede, L., Terry, R., & Hunter, J. (2015). Ethnographic evaluations on coverage of hard-to-count minority in the US decennial censuses. In R. Tourangeau, B. Edwards, T. P. Johnson, K. M. Wolter, & N. Bates (Eds.), *Hart-to-survey populations* (pp. 293–315). Cambridge: Cambridge University Press.

Simpson, L., & Middleton, E. (1997). *Who is missed by a national census? A review of empirical results from Australia, Britain, Canada, and the USA.* UK: The Cathie Marsh Centre for Census and Survey Research, University of Manchester.

Taylor, P., Lopez, M. H., Passel, J., & Motel, S. (2011). *Unauthorized immigrants: length of residency, patterns of parenthood.* Washington DC: Pew Research Center.

The Annie E. Casey Foundation. (2012). *Data snapshot on high poverty communities.* Baltimore, MD: The Annie E. Casey Foundation.

U.S. Bureau of Labor Statistics. (2011). *American time use survey-2010 results.* New Release USDL-11-0919, U.S. Bureau of Labor Statistics, Washington, DC.

U.S. Census Bureau. (2011). For people with age imputed see 2010 Census Table P49 obtained from American Factfinder.

U.S. Census Bureau. (2012a). *DSSD 2010 Census Coverage Measurement Memorandum Series #2010-G-02.* 2010 Census Coverage Measurement Estimation Report: Summary of Estimates of Coverage for Housing Units in the United States, May 22, 2012, U.S. Census Bureau, Washington, DC.

U.S. Census Bureau. (2012b). *DSSD 2010 census coverage measurement memorandum series #2010-G-04.* 2010 Census Coverage Measurement Estimation Report: Components of Census Coverage for the Household Population in the United States. U.S. Census Bureau, Washington, DC.

U.S. Census Bureau. (2014a). *Planning database with 2010 census and 2008–2012 American community survey data: At the tract level.* Washington, DC: U.S. Census Bureau. (Available online at).

U.S. Census Bureau. (2014b). *Poverty neighborhoods changes in areas with concentrated poverty: 2000 to 2010.* American Community Survey Reports, ACS-27, U.S. Census Bureau, Washington, DC.

U.S. Census Bureau. (2015, January 2015). *Current population survey, 2014 annual social and economic supplement.* Internet Release.

U.S. Federal Interagency Forum on Child and Families Statistics. (2013). America's Children, Key Indicators of Well-Being, Table FAM4.

Walejko, G. K., Miller, P. V., & Bates, N. (2011). Modeling intended 2010 census participation. Paper delivered at the American Association of Public Opinion Research conference, Phoenix, AZ, May 30, 2011.

West, K. K., & Fein, D. J. (1990). Census undercounts: An historical and contemporary sociological issue. *Sociological Inquiry, 60*(2), 127–141.

West, K., & Robinson, J. G. (1999). *What do we know about the undercount or children?* U.S. Census Bureau, Population Division working paper, U.S. Census Bureau, Washington, DC.

Wetrogan, S. I., & Crease, A. R. (2001). *ESCAP II, characteristics of imputations.* Report no. 22, U.S. Census Bureau, Washington, DC.

Word, D. L. (1997). *Who responds/who doesn't? Analyzing variation in mail response rates during the 1990 census.* Population Division Working Paper No. 19, U.S. Census Bureau, Washington, DC.

Yosikawa, H., Kholoptseva, J., & Suarez-Orozco, C. (2014). The role of public policies and community based organizations in the developmental consequences of parent undocumented status. *Social Policy Report, 27*(3). (Society for Research on Child Development).

Chapter 8
Summary and Conclusions

In this chapter I review the key findings and offer a few closing comments with respect to the 2020 U.S. Decennial Census. Readers are reminded that there is a summary at the end of every chapter.

8.1 Key Results from This Study

- The Demographic Analysis method provides more accurate estimates for the net undercount of young children than does the Dual Systems Estimate methodology.
- The net Census coverage rate for the total population in the 2010 U.S. Census (0.1 %) is a product of a net overcount rate of 0.7 % for adults and a 1.7 % undercount for children.
- The net undercount for children age 0–4 in the 2010 Census was 970,000 people or 4.6 %. The net undercount rate for children age 0–4 in the 2010 U.S. Census was higher than the net undercount for any other age group.
- It is important to examine young children and older children separately in Census coverage research. The net undercount rate for the population age 0–4 (4.6 %) was substantially higher than any other age group of children. In contrast to the net undercount rate for young children, the population age 14–17 had a net overcount rate of 1.4 %.
- Consistent with much of the Census undercount literature, the net undercount rates for young Blacks Alone or in Combination and Hispanics were higher than average. The net undercount for Hispanics age 0–4 (7.5 %) and for Black Alone or in Combination age 0–4 (6.3 %) were more than twice as high as the rate for the Not Black Alone or in Combination not Hispanic (a proxy for Non-Hispanic Whites) which experienced an estimated net undercount of 2.7 %.
- From 1950 to 1980, the net undercount rates of all children and young children were similar to those of adults and all undercount rates decreased. However, after 1980 the rates diverged. The net undercount rate for young children increased from 1.4 % in the 1980 U.S. Census to 4.6 % in the 2010 U.S.

© The Author(s) 2015
W.P. O'Hare, *The Undercount of Young Children in the U.S. Decennial Census,*
SpringerBriefs in Population Studies, DOI 10.1007/978-3-319-18917-8_8

Census. The net undercount rates for adults went from a small net undercount in the 1980 Census to a small net overcount in the 2010 Census.

- The net undercount rate for young children in the 2010 U.S. Census is higher in large states and large counties. The 128 largest counties (those with populations of 500,000 or more) accounted for 77 % of the net undercount of young children although they accounted for only 50 % of the population age 0–4. The collective net undercount rate for children age 0–4 living in counties of 500,000 or more was 7.8 %.

- Many Censuses from other countries reflect a high net undercount for young children and the net undercount for young children was generally higher than the net undercount for older children. However, unlike the U.S., young children typically did not have the highest net undercount of any age group in the other countries examined in this report.

- There is a dearth of ideas in the demographic literature about why young children have a higher net undercount than older children and adults. On a host of characteristics, young children, especially young Black and Hispanic children, live in the types of neighborhoods, households and living arrangements that make them more difficult to enumerate than older children or adults. There is also evidence that young children may be left off Census questionnaire that are returned by respondents either because respondents believe data on young children is not desired, because respondent may want to conceal the existence of a young children from government authorities, or because young children are typically listed last on Census questionnaires and some households do not complete the questionnaire. More research is needed on the question of why young children have such a high net undercount in the Census.

8.2 Looking Forward to the 2020 U.S. Census

Given the high net undercount of young children in past Censuses, it is important to ask what can be done to get a more complete count of young children in the 2020 U.S. Census. How can we reach the adults in households where young children live and motivate them to complete Census questionnaires and include all children in the household?

The time to identify causes for the high net undercount of young children and develop plans to remedy this long-standing problem in the 2020 Census is limited. According to the Census Bureau plans (2014), the main research and testing phase for the 2020 Census will end in 2015. There are opportunities for limited research in 2016 and 2017, but this is largely a time for designing 2020 Census operations. The Census Bureau's Task Force on the Undercount of Young Children (Griffin 2014, p. i) noted this situation and concluded, "Testing in the next few years should reflect a greater understanding of how to reduce this undercount."

Perhaps the most important suggestion regarding the 2020 Census is to make sure the professionals at the Census Bureau who are in charge of designing experiments, collecting data, and/or administering programs are aware of the high net undercount of children. In discussing the high net undercount of young children, the report from the Census Bureau's Task Force on the Net Undercount of Young Children (Griffin 2014, p. I) concluded,

> Staff working on 2020 Planning need to ensure that development work this decade includes a more conscious effort to address this problem. Testing in the next few years should reflect a greater understanding of how to reduce this undercount.

Despite the paucity of attention given the high net undercount of young children, in the past, this topic it is not a new issue. The U.S. Census Bureau's Task Force on the Net Undercount of Young Children (Griffin 2014, p. i) concluded "This is not a new problem and has been present in Decennial Censuses for many decades." Under-reporting of young children is also seen in many major Census Bureau surveys and in Censuses in many other countries.

As we move toward the 2020 Census, the Census Bureau has recognized the high net undercount of young children as an important topic and is taking steps to address this issue. A recent announcement by the Census Bureau indicates that they plan to devote special attention to the issue (Vitrano 2014),

> In addition, I plan to identify a point person for this specific issue – improving the coverage of young children in official statistics. This individual will serve as an advocate for high quality data for young children and work with both Census and demographic survey managers to understand and address the causes for this undercount.

In January of 2015, the Census Bureau named senior Census Bureau researcher Patrick Cantwell to head up the initiative on the undercount of young children. As this manuscript is being written, the Census Bureau is organizing staff to work on the issue. It is also noteworthy that in February of 2015, the Census Bureau gave the Census Bureau Task Force on the Undercount of Young Children a Bronze Award for outstanding work on this issue. These steps suggests that the Census Bureau sees the undercount of young children as a high priority as we move toward the 2020 Decennial Census.

I don't think I can provide any better closing comments that the quote below from The U.S. Census Task Force on the Undercount of Young Children (Griffin 2014, p. 20),

> The undercount of children under age five in the Decennial Census, and in surveys like the ACS, is real and growing. The methods employed in 2010 did not address this undercount in ways that might have been possible and the 2010 research and evaluation program provides no formal or even informal assessments of the likely causes. This needs to change as we approach 2020. Census Bureau managers need to understand and communicate the reality of this problem with staff responsible for data collection operations in both the Census and in surveys such as the ACS.

References

Griffin, D. H. (2014). *Final task force report. Task force on the undercount of young children.* Memorandum for Frank A. Vitrano, U.S. Census Bureau, Washington, DC, February 2.

U.S. Census Bureau. (2014). *2020 Census planning.* Washington, DC: U.S. Census Bureau.

Vitrano, F. (2014). *Counting young children in censuses and surveys.* Blog for Associate Director for 2020 Census. Washington, DC: U.S. Census Bureau.